MrMmm...

A taste of Belizean cooking

CUBOLA BOOKS / BELIZE

Published by Cubola Productions
35 Elizabeth Street
Benque Viejo del Carmen
Belize, C.A.

First Edition April 2003
Second Edition April 2004
Third Edition September 2005

Editor: Tracey Brown de Langan
Design: A to Z Graphic Studio
Cover painting by Mary O´Connor
Printed and bound in México

ISBN 976-8161-0-51

Acknowledgements

The recipes in this book were generously supplied by hotels and restaurants around Belize. We hope their publication here will bring many hours of enjoyment, from planning menus, selecting ingredients and preparing these delicious dishes, to eating them with friends and loved ones.

In addition to the wealth of traditional Belizean fare, there are many cooks who are combining local and imported ingredients in innovative ways, inspiring us all to new culinary heights. The recipes we received have proven this beyond a shadow of a doubt. We are most grateful to each of the contributors listed below.

Our hearty thanks go out to all of the chefs, restauranteurs and hoteliers across Belize who generously contributed their recipes and their time to this cookbook.

We would also like to thank Felicia Nuñez for the use of recipes from her wonderful book, *Tidewese Nanigi Lumagien Niregigi, Gifts From My Heart and My Firehearth*. Her stories and insights into Garifuna and Belizean life are as interesting as her recipes are delicious.

The art students of St. John's College, under the guidance of Yasser Musa, allowed us to use their delightful prints for the book's illustrations. Many thanks to these promising artists: Arlan Bennett, Javier Bosch, Lennox Cayetano, Lindberg Graham, Noel Leal, Keren Moaney, Amy Sheng, Thomas Stark and Floyd Sutherland. Our gratitude and appreciation to Gilvano Swasey for his skillful printing of the images.

Our heartfelt thanks to all concerned.

Thank you!

Caesar's Place, Cayo

Café Sol, San Ignacio, Cayo

Caladium Restaurant, Belmopan

Jennie Staines, Caliente!, San Pedro, Ambergris Caye

Chef Sean Beaton, Catering by Design, Gales Point Manatee

Masanori Kondo, Cayo Centre for Employment Training, San Ignacio

Robert Argue, Chaa Creek Cottages, Cayo

Chan Chich Lodge, Gallon Jug

duPlooy's Restaurant, Cayo

Elvi's Kitchen, San Pedro, Ambergris Caye

Fido's Courtyard & Pier, San Pedro, Ambergris Caye

Five Sisters Lodge, Cayo

Franco's Restaurant, Luba Hati, Placencia Penninsula

Ilda Garcia, Ilda's Catering, San Ignacio, Cayo

Bill Altman, Kitty's Place, Placencia

Kenrick Theus, Lamanai Outpost Lodge, Indian Church, Orange Walk

Macy's Café, Belize City and Macy's Café II, San Ignacio, Cayo

Suzi Mickler, Maya Mountain Lodge, San Ignacio, Cayo

Pamella Picon, Mopan River Resort, Benque Viejo, Cayo

New Joker Restaurant, Belize City

Felicia Nuñez from her book *Gifts From My Heart and My Firehearth*

Theo Cocchi, Parrot Nest Lodge, Bullet Tree Falls, Cayo

Pooks Hill Kitchen, Roaring River, Cayo

Ahmet Arslan, Princess Hotel and Casino, Belize City

Jose Ortiz, Ramon's Village, San Pedro

Glen Schwendinger, Rendezvous Restaurant and Winery, North Ambergris Caye

Mariam Bedran Roberson, San Ignacio Resort Hotel, Cayo

San Pedro Holiday Hotel, Ambergris Caye

Sanny's Grill, San Ignacio, Cayo

Seaside Cabañas, Caye Caulker

Mrs. Dahlia Castillo, Tony's Inn & Beach Resort, Corozal Town

Chef Whiz, Tranquility Lodge, Jacintoville, Toledo

Upstairs Pollito Dorado, San Ignacio, Cayo

Chef Maurice, Wish Willy Bar and Grill

Yoli's Pizza & Ice Cream Shoppe, San Ignacio, Cayo

Anansi cooks dinner

Table of Contents

Vegetarian Dishes (From the Garden)

Sol Soyburgers *51*

Cassava Soufflé *52*

Spaghetti Anto's Style *53*

Cho-cho with Spaghetti and Cilantro *54*

Stuffed Chayote *55*

Stuffed Green Pepper *56*

Hunkar Begendi (Grilled Eggplant with Cheese) *57*

Broiled Polenta with Portobello Mushrooms *58*

Baked Sweet Potato *59*

Stewed Pumpkin with Ground Sesame Seeds *60*

Green Papaya Casserole *61*

Spinach Cakes *62*

Curried Green Bananas *63*

Tamalitos (Dukunu) *64*

Jennie's Mexican Rice *65*

Jalapeño Rice *66*

Main Dishes (From the Land)

Norwegian Beef Salad *68*

Pork with Chipotle Honey Glaze *69*

Sanny's Pork Chops *70*

Ginger Pork *71*

Rice and Beans with Coconut Milk *72*

Stewed Chicken *73*

Fried Chicken with Onion Sauce *74*

Cashew Chicken *75*

Chicken Pibil *76-77*

Macy's Curry Chicken *78*

Escabeche *79*

Yogurt Ginger Chicken *80*

Roman Chicken *81*

Stewed Beef *82*

Spiced Beef Tenderloin with Mango Salsa *83*

Chorizo and Egg Burritos *84*

Black Bean Combo *85*

Meatballs Wrapped in Cabbage Leaves *86*

Breadfruit Meat or Fish Rolls *87*

Spicy Mango Curry Sauce *88*

Orange Onion Balsamic Sauce *89*

Main Dishes (From the Sea)

Snapper Caribe *91*

Seafood Lasagna *92-93*

Fish with Cashew Sauce *94*

Fish Escabeche *95*

Introduction

by Karla Heusner

I have a terrible confession: I don't know how to make rice and beans. What! An yu live ina Belize so long??! Yes, it's true, although my Belizean grandma, "Miss Julia", made some of the most delicious rice and beans you can imagine, there must have been some genetic accident when I was conceived. Yes, tragically, I find myself without the necessary Belizean rice-and-beans gene. My attempts are so bad, not even the neighborhood stray dog can wuff it down without giving me a look of reproach. Imagine a pot not even a "potlicker" dog wants!

Until now I have kept my deficiency a secret, impressing my family and friends with other dishes. But when I got an advanced copy of *Mmmmmm! A Taste of Belizean Cooking*, I saw there was a recipe for rice and beans with coconut milk in the "Main Dishes" section. So here I am, pot boiling away as I write this with high hopes of success... this time. I'll let you know how it turns out in a bit.

In the meantime, let's talk about cooking, and cookbooks. If you are not one of those people who simply throw ingredients together (without measuring of course) and make miraculous things happen, you probably lean heavily on cookbooks; and this is certainly a lovely cookbook to lean on.

As you noticed while flipping through the pages before you bought it, this is not your typical cruise through Belizean cuisine. I think you will agree it retains the basic foods we all know and love while pushing our culinary arts to a new level. The recipes so generously shared by the various contributors may take your cooking to a new level too. For obviously, if you bought this book you are not one of those who every Sunday has to have your rice-and-beans-and-chicken-and-salad (said as one word, in a breathless rush). No, YOU are more daring, more experimental. You will be willing to take an old favorite and give it a new face; you will be eager to use Belizean products in a new way. For you, shrimps do not merely sit atop chow mein at your neighborhood take-out. No, they can be enhanced with coconut batter or even feta cheese. You might even consider putting shrimp and goat cheese together in tamales. Talk about unconventional!

In this book you will find the time honored classics like Conch Soup and Black Bean Soup. But how about trying Carrot Ginger Soup? Or Calaloo with Shrimp Soup? Now those are conversation starters. Speaking of Belizean vegetables, there could be a whole chapter in this book called the "the amazing cho-cho." For this hardy vegetable can be pickled and served in a bean salad or added to spaghetti and cilantro. You can even stuff them for an interesting variation on that old stand-by, stuffed peppers.

What I like most about the book is that it has the recipes for the things you love when other people make them and now you can make them yourself. Specifically I am referring to Dukunu and Escabeche, or even Macy's Curry Chicken. At the same time, the cookbook definitely has an exotic flair with Curried Green Bananas and Kibi or Roman Chicken. Aren't the dessert and drinks sections delectable? I may be a bit "main meal" challenged, but desserts are something I can pull off with panache. Now you can too. Besides banana bread, you can make banana cake, or put your bananas in custard sauce or caramel. Who needs apple crisp or peach cobbler when you can do it with coconuts and mangoes? Despite the fact that my grandma made the *most* heavenly lime pie (which I can only assume she is now making in heaven for the angels themselves) I am willing to try this particular recipe to see how it measures up to hers. For this is how we cook, isn't it? Always comparing how our meals come out compared to someone else's. We share recipes, altering them slightly—either by accident or design—to create delicious variations. And if we are lucky, our children, or grandchildren remember our specialties with such fondness they later call us to ask how to make them for their own families. So, like our languages, our cuisine evolves and changes, getting richer over time. Fortunately, for today's Belizeans cooks, our suppliers have evolved a bit too. These days we are no longer restricted by a limited range of tinned products crammed on the shelves of tiny shops. You won't have to stand there waiting patiently as things are measured and bagged off or be disappointed by the response "No, we no gat dat." For you will find that the ingredients for these recipes can be found at your local supermarket, and the fresh items and produce at your local street market or vegetable stand. The recipes use the best Belize has to offer, in an eclectic mix of ethnic styles and ingredients, like our very society. Just as our families welcome a new child by simply adding another potspoonful of rice to the pot, our cooks always welcome another visitor to the table. With no fuss. You will welcome these recipes to your collection of favorite things to "whip up," to serve at dinner parties, to your friends and family, or even to enjoy by yourself if you can steal some precious time away. So whether you have been looking for the perfect coconut pie, (just like the one you ate at the caye that time), to comfort your friends with coffee, or mesmerize them with your margaritas, this is the book for you. Don't worry, the recipes work. I took the Hummus, the Marinated Tomato Salad, the Chorizo and Egg Burritos, and the Escabeche for test rides. Not all in one day mind you, but I did pull them off. Everything tasted great and at no time did the kitchen catch fire and there were no injuries. So now, I know you are wondering: "How the rice and beans turn out?" Hold on, let me check... Well, they look like rice and beans, and what's more, they taste like rice and beans! So maybe I am saved, the curse is lifted (as long as I follow the recipe every time and don't get overconfident I guess). So what will you cook this Sunday? Will you succumb to the pressure of a parent or spouse who sits down at the table during "rice hours" and asks where the rice is? You could just say it's in this cookbook under Mexican Rice or Fancy Rice Salad as you blissfully chop, sift and sing, an open copy of *Mmmmmm! A Taste of Belizean Cooking* next to you. Buen provecho!

Appetizers

Champagne Herb Grouper
with Mushrooms

by Chef Sean Beaton, Catering by Design, Gales Point Manatee

Ingredients

1 lb. grouper (any firm-fleshed white fish can be substituted)
$2^2/3$ cups shredded mozzarella
1 cup mushrooms (porcini if available), sliced
2 teaspoons rosemary
2 teaspoons oregano
1 cup champagne
4 cloves garlic, chopped
1 teaspoon butter
salt and pepper to taste
1 tomato, sliced for garnish
French bread, thinly sliced and toasted

Preparation

• Pre-heat oven to 350°F (177°C)
• Rub the inside of four ramekins, or very small casseroles, liberally with butter
• Place a layer of shredded mozzarella, then mushrooms, garlic, salt and pepper
• Finely chop fish and mix with herbs and top the casseroles with this mixture
• Add champagne ($1/4$ cup in each ramekin)
• Bake for 15 minutes and remove casseroles from oven
• Place a small plate over casseroles a turn over onto plates
• Garnish with sliced tomatoes if desired and serve with toasted French bread

Serves 4

Coconut Shrimp
with Honey Mustard

by Chef Sean Beaton, Catering by Design, Gales Point Manatee

Ingredients

1 cup flaked coconut
1 egg
$^3/4$ cup milk
$^1/2$ teaspoon baking powder
$^1/2$ cup flour
1 coconut halved (optional)
6 medium to large shrimp, peeled and de-veined
cooking oil for deep frying
2 teaspoons mustard (Dijon preferably)
$^1/4$ cup rainforest honey (or any honey)

Preparation

- In a bowl combine egg, milk, baking powder and flour
- In a separate bowl or plate spread Angel Flake coconut
- In a small saucepan or deep fryer heat oil until hot, about 375-400°F (190-204°C)
- Dip shrimp into egg mixture, then into coconut flake
- Deep fry until golden brown
- In a halved coconut or soup cup combine honey and mustard as a dipping sauce
- Drain oil from shrimp on a paper towel, arrange on plate with dipping sauce, serve warm (not hot)

Serves 2

Conch Fritters

by Mrs. Dahlia Castillo, Tony's Inn & Beach Resort, Corozal Town

Ingredients

1 lb. conch
1/2 sweet pepper, minced
1/2 habanero pepper (no seeds)
1/2 tomato, diced finely
1/4 onion, minced
juice of 1 lime
sprig cilantro
dash salt and pepper
2 cups flour
2 teaspoons baking powder
1 cup water
1/3 cup vegetable oil

Pico de Gallo :
Combine diced tomatoes, onions, cilantro, salt and pepper to taste, lime juice and a dash of olive oil.

Preparation

• Clean and dice conch and place in food processor with vegetables and lime juice
• Pulse until fine and well mixed together
• If no food processor is available, beat conch to tenderize, and then mince
• Add to minced vegetables with salt and pepper to taste, mixing well
• Combine dry ingredients together and add processed conch and vegetables
• Mix well, adding water to moisten
• Drop by tablespoonful into hot oil and cook until golden
• Remove from oil and drain on paper towel

Serves 8

Note
For cocktail servings cook using teaspoonful instead of tablespoonful. Can be served with salsa or Pico de Gallo.

Kibi

by Mariam Bedran Roberson, San Ignacio Resort Hotel, Cayo

Ingredients

1 cup cracked wheat (bulghur)
1 lb. finely ground lamb (beef can be subsituted for lamb)
1 1/2 teaspoons salt
1 teaspoon black pepper
2 tablespoons olive oil
3 cloves garlic
dash of hot sauce to taste
1/2 teaspoon cinnamon
1/2 teaspoon ground allspice
1/4 cup mint leaves, chopped
1/4 cup basil leaves, chopped
oil for deep frying

Preparation

• Place wheat in bowl and cover with water
• Let soak at least 20-30 minutes until wheat is swollen but not too soft
• Drain wheat and squeeze out all excess water
• Add wheat to ground lamb and knead until well mixed
• Add all other ingredients and mix well
• Form mixture into round, egg shaped balls, deep fry in hot oil until golden brown
• Test the first batch to ensure that it is cooked through, but do not over fry or wheat will become hard
• Enjoy these delicious kibi with hummus and hot flour tortillas

Serves 4

Note
Kibi can be served either as an entrée or appetizer. Recipe may be doubled or tripled as needed.

Hummus

by Mariam Bedran Roberson, San Ignacio Resort Hotel, Cayo

Ingredients

1 can (17 ounce) garbanzo beans, drained
5 tablespoons prepared tahini sauce (sesame paste available in specialty shops)
1/2 cup water
4 cloves garlic
1 teaspoon salt
1/2 teaspoon black pepper
4 tablespoons lime juice
4-5 large mint leaves

Preparation

- Place all above ingredients (except garbanzos) in blender and process until smooth
- Add garbanzos slowly and process until all beans have been mixed and blended in well
- Pour into serving dish and garnish with a little olive oil and mint leaves
- Serve with flour tortillas and kibi

Note
These recipes, which originated within our family's Lebanese history and culture are courtesy of the Bedran family, owners of the San Ignacio Resort Hotel.

Serves 4 to 5

Country Frittata

by Masanori Kondo, Cayo Centre for Employment Training, San Ignacio

Ingredients

6 eggs
1 medium onion
2 potatoes
1/2 cup cooked bacon
1/2 zucchini
2 tablespoons Parmesan cheese
1 teaspoon butter
2 tablespoons olive oil
1/2 cup tomato sauce
parsley
salt and black pepper

Preparation

- Cut zucchini, potato, onion, and bacon into cubes
- Boil potato for 5 minutes then drain well
- In a frying pan cook bacon over medium low heat
- Add onion to the pan, then zucchini and potato and season with additional salt and black pepper as needed then spread on a plate to cool
- Beat eggs in a bowl and add Parmesan cheese and mix well
- Add vegetables and mix together
- Heat olive oil and butter in a frying pan over medium flame
- Put egg and vegetable mixture in the pan and stir it until it begins to set
- Let it cook over low flame until the surface has set
- Cover it with a flat plate and turn the frying pan over to put the mixture on the plate
- Heat butter in the frying pan and return the mixture to the frying pan
- Fry it for a few minutes
- Cut the frittata into wedges and serve it with tomato sauce

Serves 4 to 8

Vegetable Spring Rolls

by Masanori Kondo, Cayo Centre for Employment Training, San Ignacio

Ingredients

1/4 small cabbage
1/4 carrot
1 onion
2 ribs celery
cilantro (if desired)
3 dried mushrooms
12 spring roll wrappers (rice paper, usually available in Chinese supermarkets)

Seasoning:
1 tablespoon rum
2 tablespoons soy sauce
1/2 cup chicken stock
1 pinch sugar
1 pinch black pepper
2 tablespoons corn starch in water
1 teaspoon sesame oil (or vegetable oil)
1/4 cup flour mixed with water to make paste

Dipping Sauces:
In a small bowl mix:
1/2 cup soy sauce
1/2 cup vinegar
Place in another small bowl:
3 tablespoons ketchup
1 tablespoon mustard

Paste Mixture:
1/4 cup flour mixed with water to make paste

Preparation

- Soak dried mushrooms in warm water until reconstituted
- Slice cabbage, carrot, onion, celery and dried mushrooms into thin strips
- Chop cilantro and mix with seasoning ingredients in a bowl
- Heat a pan with 1 tablespoon oil and fry vegetables
- Add seasoning mixture to vegetables and when finished frying, spread on a plate to cool
- Place small amount of filling on one end of a spring roll wrapper
- Fold in triangles, securing final edge with the paste mixture
- Deep fry at 350°F (177°C) until golden brown
- Serve with dipping sauces mixed to taste

Serves 4

Rendezvous Ceviche

by G. Schwendinger, Rendezvous Restaurant and Winery, North Ambergris Caye

Ingredients

1 fresh fish fillet (8-12 ounces)
4-6 tablespoons shallot vinegar
2 tablespoons olive oil
salt and pepper to taste
1/2 red onion, finely diced
1/2 tomato, finely diced
1/2 teaspoon dried chilies
4 sprigs cilantro

Preparation

• Combine vinegar, oil, salt, pepper and fine mirepoix of diced tomato and red onions and mix well
• Slice fish thinly across the fillet and add to mixture
• Let sit 3-5 hours turning occasionally to coat
• Sprinkle with chilies and cilantro to serve

Serves 4 to 6

Colleen's Pâté

by G. Schwendinger, Rendezvous Restaurant and Winery, North Ambergris Caye

Ingredients

1 lb. chicken livers
1/2 red onion
4 tablespoons butter
2 1/2 cups (1/2 lb.) mushrooms
14-20 basil leaves
1 teaspoon curry powder
1 teaspoon paprika
1 teaspoon each, salt and pepper
1/4 teaspoon turmeric
2 tablespoons cognac

Preparation

• Slice mushrooms and onions into small pieces
• De-nerve chicken livers (cut out the thin white colored vein between the left and right sides of the liver using a paring knife)
• Sauté the above with 2 teaspoons butter and spices until livers are cooked, about 10 minutes
• Add cognac and allow mixture to cool
• Place in blender with basil leaves, add remaining butter and blend until smooth
• Pour into a loaf pan lined with foil
• Cool and refrigerate 3-4 hours

Serves 10 to 12

Salsa and Cheese Biscuits

by duPlooy's Restaurant, Cayo

Ingredients

3 cups white flour
1 teaspoon salt
4 teaspoons baking soda
3/4 cup butter or margarine
1/4 cup grated cheese
1 1/2 cups Salsa Casera
(available in shops or use this recipe)

Preparation

- Pre-heat oven to 425°F (218°C)
- Sift together flour, salt and baking soda
- Cut butter into flour until it resembles fine meal
- Stir in grated cheese and add salsa casera
- Gently knead only until mixed into flour
- Turn onto a floured counter and roll to 1/4-1/2 inch high and cut into rounds with biscuit cutter or upside down cup
- Place biscuits on ungreased cookie sheet with edges touching
- Bake for about 15 minutes until tops begin to brown
- Serve hot

Makes 18-24 biscuits

Salsa Casera

2 tomatoes, finely diced
1/2 green pepper, finely diced
1/2 onion, finely diced
1 clove garlic, minced and crushed
1/2 habanero pepper with seeds, diced
juice of 1 lemon
1/2 teaspoon salt

Combine all ingredients except salt and let sit for 1 hour. Add salt. Can be used in recipes or as a side dish.

Italian Bread

by Theo Cocchi, Parrot Nest Lodge, Bullet Tree Falls, Cayo

Ingredients

3 cups flour
3 tablespoons sugar
$1^1/2$ tablespoons mixed Italian seasonings (oregano, thyme, basil, etc...)
$1/2$ cup grated Parmesan cheese
12 ounces ($1^1/2$ cups) beer, at room temperature
3 tablespoons soft butter or margarine
3 tablespoons cornmeal

Preparation

• In a mixing bowl, mix together the first 4 ingredients, with an electric or hand mixer
• Mix in the beer and butter
• Grease loaf pan and dust with cornmeal
• Pour batter into loaf pan and dust the top with remaining cornmeal
• Bake at 325°F (163°C) for 1 hour

Makes 1 loaf

SOUPS

Tomato Lime Soup

by duPlooy's Restaurant, Cayo

Ingredients

3 garlic cloves, pressed
$1^1/2$ teaspoons cumin
1 tablespoon olive oil
6 cups tomato juice
2 cups fresh tomatoes
juice from $1^1/2$ limes
$^1/4$ teaspoon cinnamon
$^1/2$ teaspoon salt
$^1/4$ teaspoon black pepper
3 tablespoons fresh chopped cilantro
$^1/4$ teaspoon mild hot sauce
tortilla chips for garnish

Preparation

• Sauté garlic and cumin in olive oil until soft
• Add tomato juice, tomatoes, lime juice, cinnamon, salt and pepper
• Simmer for 10 minutes, then turn off heat and stir in cilantro and hot sauce
• Serve topped with crushed tortillas chips and chopped cilantro

Serves 6

Black-Eyed Pea Soup

by Pooks Hill Kitchen, Roaring River, Cayo

Ingredients

1 lb. black-eyed peas
3 onions
3 cloves garlic
1 tablespoon turmeric
1 chili pepper, chopped
1 tablespoon tomato paste
salt and pepper
lime juice
cilantro

Preparation

• Cook black-eyed peas in large covered pan until tender (about 3/4 hour)
• Remove from pan with liquid
• Heat oil and add chopped onions, garlic, chili, turmeric and tomato paste
• Add beans and liquid
• Continue cooking for 20 minutes
• Add cilantro, salt and pepper and a squeeze of lime juice
• Serve hot with tortillas

Serves 8

AVocado and Chicken Soup

by Felicia Nuñez from her book Gifts From My Heart and My Firehearth

Ingredients

6 cups chicken broth (or bouillon)
1 chicken, cut in pieces, seasoned
1 medium onion, sliced
2 firm, ripe avocados, cubed
2 cloves garlic, chopped
1 large carrot, in small cubes
1/4 cup chopped cilantro
1/2 hot pepper, chopped
1/2 lb. white cheese, cubed
1 teaspoon lime juice
3 tablespoons butter
3 tablespoons oil

Preparation

- Bring the broth to a boil and put the seasoned chicken in it
- Simmer until chicken is tender
- Remove and cool on a plate, then take chicken off the bones
- Heat oil in a heavy skillet and cook onion, garlic, carrot cubes and chopped pepper
- Add to chicken broth with butter, chicken, lime juice and cheese cubes
- Drop avocado cubes into the soup and cook just until all is heated through and cheese is melted

Serves 4

Fish and Okra Soup

by Felicia Nuñez from her book Gifts From My Heart and My Firehearth

Ingredients

6 cups beef broth (or beef bouillon)
2 onions, sliced
2 large carrots, cubed
1 stalk celery, chopped
2 teaspoons cilantro
$1/2$ teaspoon black pepper
$1/2$ teaspoon salt
1 lb. boneless fish, well seasoned with seasoning salt and recado
2 lbs. okra
1 small tin tomato sauce

Preparation

• Place beef broth in a large cooking pot with onions, carrots, celery and seasonings
• Simmer for 15 minutes
• Cut fish meat into small pieces and cook in broth until fish becomes flaky
• Cook okra separately then mash or purée in a blender
• Add okra and tomato sauce and heat thoroughly

Serves 4

Drunken Beans

by Kenrick Theus, Lamanai Outpost Lodge, Indian Church, Orange Walk

Ingredients

3/4 lb. bacon slices, chopped
3 large onions, chopped
4 lbs. cooked pinto beans, drained
3 bottles beer
3 cups beef broth
3 large tomatoes chopped
1 1/2 cups fresh cilantro, chopped
3 jalapenos, diced
1 tablespoon sugar

Preparation

• Cook bacon in a heavy pot until crisp
• Add onion and sauté until soft
• Add all other ingredients
• Season with salt and black pcppcr
• Reduce heat and allow to simmer
• Serve in small bowls

Serves 4

Note
Can be made a day ahead to allow flavors to blend properly.

Curried Peanut Soup

by Robert Argue, Chaa Creek Cottages, Cayo

Ingredients

1 cup plain peanut butter
2 tablespoons honey
4 cups boiling water
1-2 tablespoons peanut oil
2 cups onion, minced
10 large cloves garlic, minced
2 teaspoons salt
2-3 tablespoons fresh ginger, minced
2 cups buttermilk (room temperature)

Spice Mixture:
1 teaspoon cinnamon
2 teaspoons ground coriander
1 teaspoon ground cardamom
1/2 teaspoon ground cloves
2 teaspoons turmeric
1 tablespoon ground cumin
1 teaspoon dry mustard
up to 1/2 teaspoon cayenne

Note: the spice mixture can be replaced with 2 tablespoons of curry powder.

Preparation

• Place the peanut butter and honey in a medium-sized bowl
• Add about 2 cups of the boiling water and mash with a spoon until it becomes a smooth paste
• Whisk in the remaining hot water and set aside
• Heat the oil in a soup pot or Dutch oven
• Add the onions, garlic, salt, and ginger
• Sauté for about 10 minutes over medium heat then add the spice mixture
• Continue to cook and stir for about 5 minutes more
• Stir in the peanut butter mixture and cover
• Bring to a boil then turn the heat way down, and simmer for about 20 minutes, stirring occasionally
• Just before serving, whisk in the room temperature buttermilk
• Serve hot

Serves 6 to 8

Calaloo With Shrimp Soup

by Franco's Restaurant, Luba Hati, Placencia Penninsula

Ingredients

bunch of calaloo (amaranth) leaves chopped into small pieces or into a chiffonade
1 tablespoon olive oil
1/2 inch piece of fresh ginger, minced
2 cloves garlic, minced
2 stems of lemon grass (fever grass) peeled of all outer leaves and lightly crushed
1/2 glass of white wine
1 quart (4 cups) fish or chicken stock
dash of soy sauce or fish sauce (optional)
16 medium shrimp
salt and cayenne pepper to taste

Preparation

• Sauté ginger, garlic and lemon grass in oil for a minute or so
• Add calaloo and stir for a couple of minutes
• Add wine and let greens wilt
• Add stock and bring to boil
• Remove and discard lemon grass stalk
• Add shrimp and soy sauce and continue cooking for one more minute
• The soup should be clear and flavorful, do not overload with greens

Serves 4

Conch Soup

by Macy's Cafe II, San Ignacio, Cayo

Ingredients

2 lbs. conch
1 tablespoons butter
1 sweet pepper, diced
1 tomato, diced
1 onion, diced
1/2 teaspoon garlic, minced
salt and pepper to taste

If desired you can add:
3 lbs. coco, peeled and cubed
1 lb. okra, with tops cut off
• Boil together for about 10 minutes
• Add to conch soup

Preparation

• Clean conch, beat and cut into small pieces
• Boil or pressure cook until soft, about 1 hour
• Sauté sweet pepper, tomato, onion and garlic in butter
• Cover with foil and steam 5-10 minutes until soft
• Add conch and cover, steam for 2 minutes
• Add salt and pepper to taste
• Serve with white rice

Serves 4

carrot Ginger Soup

by Café Sol, San Ignacio, Cayo

Ingredients

$1^{1}/2$ lbs. carrots
$1/2$ lb. potatoes
1 tablespoon oil or butter
1 cup onions, chopped
3 cloves garlic
2 tablespoons fresh ginger, grated
$1^{1}/2$ teaspoons salt
$4^{1}/2$ cups water
2 teaspoons orange juice
2 teaspoons lime juice
3 tablespoons cilantro, chopped

Preparation

• Peel carrots and potatoes and cut into chunks
• Boil in water until soft
• Meanwhile sauté onion, garlic, ginger and salt in oil for 10 minutes on low heat
• Add to carrots and potatoes with orange juice and lime juice
• Mix in blender until puréed
• Add cilantro and simmer for 10 minutes

Serves 4

Black Bean Soup

Café Sol, San Ignacio, Cayo

Ingredients

2 cups black beans, cooked in 6 cups water
2 cups onion, chopped
2 teaspoons cumin
2 teaspoons salt
black pepper to taste
5 medium cloves garlic, crushed
1 medium bell pepper, diced
1 medium carrot, diced
1 zucchini, chopped
2 medium tomatoes, diced
4 small allspice berries or 1 teaspoon ground allspice
1/2 cup orange juice
habanero sauce to taste
cilantro for garnish (optional)

Preparation

• Sauté onions with salt, pepper and cumin till soft
• Add garlic, bell pepper, carrot, zucchini, tomatoes, allspice and fry for 5 minutes
• Add to black beans - simmer for 20 minutes
• Add orange juice, habanero sauce
• Serve in bowls with cilantro sprig garnish

Serves 4

Minestrone

by Masanori Kondo, Cayo Centre for Employment Training, San Ignacio

Ingredients

1/2 onion
1/4 carrot
1 rib celery
1/2 zucchini
1 leaf cabbage
1 tomato
2 potatoes
2 tablespoons uncooked rice
1 clove garlic
4 cups water (or chicken stock)
21/2 tablespoons vegetable oil
2 tablespoons Parmesan cheese
salt and black pepper

Preparation

- Chop garlic into fine pieces
- Cut onion, carrot, celery, zucchini, cabbage, tomato, pumpkin, and potato into cubes
- Heat oil and garlic in a pot and fry garlic until fragrant
- Add onion, carrot, and celery to the pot
- Add zucchini, cabbage, and pumpkin
- Add rice, potato, salt and black pepper
- Add water (or chicken stock) to the pot and boil, lower heat and skim off any foam
- Add tomato and simmer for 15 minutes over low flame
- Season with salt and black pepper to taste
- Serve Minestrone with Parmesan cheese

Serves 4

Vegan Chowder

by Suzi Mickler. Maya Mountain Lodge, San Ignacio, Cayo

Ingredients

2 tablespoons olive oil
2 large onions, finely chopped
2 garlic cloves, minced
1 carrot, peeled and diced
4 medium potatoes, peeled and cubed
4 cups vegetable stock
1 teaspoon brown flour
1 teaspoon white flour

$2^1/2$ cups tofu milk (blend 1 pack tofu and add water to make $2^1/2$ cups)
1 sweet pepper, finely chopped
$1/3$ stalk of celery, chopped fine
1 tablespoon chopped fresh parsley
1 teaspoon lime juice
salt & pepper to taste
fresh parsley sprig for garnish

Preparation

- Fry garlic, and then add onions in 1 tablespoon oil using low heat
- Add carrot and potatoes, stirring until well mixed
- Stir in vegetable stock and bring to a boil
- Reduce heat and cook, covered, until vegetables are tender, about $1/2$ hour
- Mix remaining 1 tablespoon oil with flour
- Add 1 tablespoon drinking water and mix until smooth
- Slowly add 1 cup of the soup to the flour mixture, avoiding lumps
- Add the tofu milk to the mix and stir in well
- Pour the mix slowly into the boiling soup while stirring vigorously to avoid lumps
- Bring the soup to a boil, then immediately reduce heat to very low
- Cook 2 minutes, stirring frequently
- Add sweet pepper, celery, and parsley, and cook over low heat for 10 minutes
- Turn off heat and add lime juice, salt and pepper to taste
- Serve with small parsley sprigs floating on top and lime wedge on the side of the plate

Serves 6

Note
Optional additions can include: millet, cooked wheat, brown rice, whole wheat noodles, dumplings, tortilla chips or strips, or thin okra slices.

Creamy Corn Soup

by Masanori Kondo, Cayo Centre for Employment Training, San Ignacio

Ingredients

6 ears corn
2 tablespoons butter
1/2 onion, sliced
1/2 carrot, sliced
1 1/2 tablespoons flour
3 1/2 cups beef or chicken stock
Bouquet of herbs
 (tie together sprigs of thyme, bay leaf and parsley)
1 1/2 cups milk
1/2 cup heavy cream
salt and pepper to taste
Garnish
1 slice of bread, cubed
olive oil (sprinkle oil over cubed bread
and bake until golden)

Preparation

- Prepare corn by removing husks and silk then slice kernels off cobs
- Melt butter in a medium saucepan over medium heat and sauté onion
  and carrot slightly
- Add flour to pan and lower heat, stirring frequently
- Pour in the stock and bring to a boil
- Add corn, salt and pepper to taste and the bouquet
- Simmer over low heat for about 20 minutes
- Remove the bouquet, pour soup into a blender and purée until smooth
- Return to saucepan, add milk and heat through but do not boil
- Add cream just before serving
- Ladle hot soup into 6-8 inch bowl, top with garnish and serve immediately

salads

Red Cabbage and
Jicama Salad

Franco's Restaurant, Luba Hati, Placencia Penninsula

Ingredients

$1/2$ red cabbage, very thinly sliced
1 jicama, peeled and julienned
2 oranges, sectioned (membrane and seeds removed)
juice of one sour orange (or equal parts lime, orange and grapefruit)
$1/2$ cup cashew halves (can substitute peanuts) and raisins
2 tablespoons olive oil
salt and pepper to taste

Preparation

• Make vinaigrette with olive oil and sour orange juice
• Toss all other ingredients except orange sections with the vinaigrette
• Add orange sections and toss gently trying not to break them
• Let marinate for $1/2$ hour before serving

Serves 4

Pickled Cho-cho
and Bean Salad

Suzi Mickler, Maya Mountain Lodge, San Ignacio, Cayo

Ingredients

1^1/2 cups red kidney beans, cooked
1^1/2 cups green beans, cooked (optional)
1^1/2 cups of any other beans, cooked
2 cups cooked salted cho-cho (chayote), thinly sliced and slightly crisp
^{1}/2 cup onion, finely chopped
^{1}/2 cup green pepper, finely chopped
^{2}/3 cup sugar
1 cup vinegar
^{1}/4 cup oil
1 teaspoon salt
1 large tomato, chopped into small pieces
lettuce leaves
tomato wedges

Mustard Dressing:
^{1}/2 cup mayonnaise
^{1}/2 cup mustard
salt and freshly ground pepper to taste

Preparation

• Combine all ingredients, except the lettuce and tomatoes, in a bowl, being careful not to mash the cho-cho, add a dash of pepper
• Marinate overnight
• Prepare mustard dressing by whisking ingredients together
• To serve place cho-cho mix on a bed of lettuce with a tomato wedge on each side
• Sprinkle chopped tomato over the top, cover and refrigerate until ready to serve
• Pour mustard dressing over salad just before serving

Serves 6

Spicy Beef Salad

by G. Schwendinger, Rendezvous Restaurant and Winery, North Ambergris Caye

Ingredients

1 lb. sirloin or good cut of beef
1/2 red onion
8 fresh mint leaves
12 basil leaves
2 cloves garlic
juice of 1 lime
1/2 teaspoon sugar
2 tablespoons fish sauce
1/2 teaspoon dried chilies

Preparation

• Cut beef into small strips, 1" x 1/4", and stir fry until medium
• Mix lime, sugar, minced garlic, chili and fish sauce in a bowl and mix to dissolve sugar
• Place cooked beef in sauce
• Garnish with basil mint and onions, mix and serve

Serves 4

Marinated Tomato Salad

by Masanori Kondo, Cayo Centre for Employment Training, San Ignacio

Ingredients

4 (medium size) tomatoes
1 red onion
1 white onion
1/2 carrot
1/2 celery
1 green pepper

Dressing:
4 tablespoons vinegar
4 tablespoons sesame oil (or olive oil)
1 tablespoon soy sauce (light)
1 1/2 tablespoons chopped garlic
1 pinch each salt and black pepper

Preparation

• Cut tomatoes into round slices
• Cut onions, and green pepper into thin slices
• Cut celery and carrot into fine strips and soak them in icy cold water so the celery and carrot become crisp
• Put vinegar, soy sauce, chopped garlic, salt and black pepper in a bowl and mix well
• Add sesame oil gradually to the bowl and mix well
• Fill in a container with half of the tomatoes, sprinkle with salt, add half of the sliced onions, and green pepper
• Add another layer of tomatoes in the container, sprinkle with salt and cover with the rest of the sliced onions and green pepper
• Put the container in the refrigerator for 30-40 minutes
• Drain the celery and carrot well
• Serve the tomato, onions and green pepper on a plate
• Put the celery and carrots on the top of the tomato

Serves 4

Vegetable Salad
With Poached Egg

by Masanori Kondo, Cayo Centre for Employment Training, San Ignacio

Ingredients

1/2 red onion
1/3 lb. scallions (green onion)
1 1/2 lbs. various kinds of leaf lettuce
cilantro for garnish
red radish
4 tablespoons croutons
1/3 lb. fresh herbs
4 eggs
1 tablespoon vinegar

Dressing:
1 tablespoon mustard
2 tablespoons wine vinegar
1/2 cup olive oil
salt and pepper

Preparation

• Cut red onion, red radish and scallion into thin round slices and soak them in water
• Clean leaf lettuce and cilantro, tear into small pieces and place in a salad bowl
• Boil water and add one tablespoon vinegar
• Crack an egg into a cup to make sure it is fresh
• Carefully place each egg in the boiling water and boil gently for 3 minutes
• Place the eggs in ice water to cool then drain well
• Put mustard, salt and black pepper in a bowl and whisk them together, adding olive oil gradually
• Drain onion and radish slices well and add to salad bowl along with croutons
• Add croutons to the salad bowl and mix together
• Serve the salad on plates along with the poached egg
• Sprinkle the dressing over the salad

Serves 4

Fancy Rice Salad

by Felicia Nuñez from her book, Gifts From My Heart and My Firehearth

Ingredients

3 cups rice, cooked and cooled
3 oranges
1/4 cup raisins
1/4 cup onion, chopped
1/2 cup jicama, chopped
1 fresh cilantro sprig, chopped
1/2 cup wongla (sesame seeds), toasted
1/2 cup orange juice
1/4 cup vegetable oil
3 tablespoons sugar
1/2 teaspoon salt

Preparation

• Toast wongla in dry, hot, iron skillet and set aside
• Peel oranges and cut orange sections into smaller pieces, saving any juice
• Combine rice, orange sections, raisins, onion, jicama and cilantro and mix well
• In a small bowl, mix any juice from cutting oranges plus 1/2 cup orange juice, oil, sugar, wongla and salt
• Pour over rice salad and mix thoroughly to distribute the dressing throughout rice
• Serve cold

Serves 4

Salad Belize

by Felicia Nuñez from her book, Gifts From My Heart and My Firehearth

Ingredients

8 cups cabbage (1 large cabbage)
4 sprigs fresh cilantro, chopped
4 tomatoes, diced
1 cucumber, chopped
3 medium mango leaves, slivered
12 lime leaves, slivered
1 garlic clove, minced
1/2 cup oil
1/3 cup vinegar
juice of 1 lime
3/4 cup brown sugar
1 teaspoon salt

Preparation

• Finely chop cabbage
• Chop cilantro using some stems
• Dice tomatoes and cucumber into small pieces
• Slice mango and lime leaves into very thin slivers
• Combine all these ingredients in a large bowl, sprinkle with salt and toss to distribute salt throughout
• In a separate bowl, mix oil, vinegar, lime juice and sugar until sugar is dissolved
• Pour over salad, mix to blend dressing all through salad
• Let it sit in the refrigerator one hour before serving

Serves 6 to 8

Salad Dressing

by Theo Cocchi, Parrot Nest Lodge, Bullet Tree Falls, Cayo

Ingredients

2 tablespoons salad vinegar
$1/4$ tablespoon dry mustard
6 tablespoons olive oil
2 cloves garlic, chopped in chunks
dash of salt and pepper

Optional:
1 tablespoon lemon juice
1 tablespoons dill

Preparation

• In a jar, mix all ingredients and shake vigorously

Serves 4

Vinaigrette Sauce

by Elvi's Kitchen, San Pedro, Ambergris Caye

Ingredients

1/2 cup oil
2 teaspoons vinegar
salt and pepper
1 clove garlic
1/2 teaspoon oregano

Preparation

• Mix all ingredients thoroughly

Serves 4

Vegetarian Dishes

From the Garden

Sol Soyburgers

by Café Sol, San Ignacio, Cayo

Ingredients

2 cups soybeans, cooked and blended
2 cloves garlic, crushed
1 medium onion, minced
1 sweet pepper, diced
1 box tofu, mashed
1 carrot, grated
1/4 cup soy sauce
1 teaspoon black pepper
1 teaspoon cumin
1 teaspoon chili powder
2 teaspoons vinegar
1 teaspoon dry mustard
2 cups dry breadcrumbs

Preparation

• Mix all ingredients thoroughly and shape into patties
• Fry in a very hot pan brushed with oil
• Turn heat down and cook 10 minutes each side
• Serve on burger buns

Serves 2 to 4

Cassava Soufflé

by Bill Altman, Kitty's Place, Placencia

Ingredients

3 lbs. cassava
1 cup (^{1}/2 lb.) butter
3 cups milk
12 egg yolks
15 egg whites

Preparation

• Peel cassava and boil in enough water to cover, until it is soft
• Let cool slightly and remove stringy center
• Melt butter in milk over low heat
• Add milk and butter to cassava while mashing (or a little at a time in food processor)
• Blend until smooth
• Beat 12 egg yolks and add to cassava, mixing well
• Beat egg whites until stiff
• Fold into cassava until it has a uniform consistency
• Place in a greased, 9" x 12" baking pan
• Bake at 350°F (177°C) for approximately 45 minutes, until puffed up and golden
• Slice and serve immediately

Serves 8

Spaghetti Anto's Style

by Caesar's Place, Cayo

Ingredients

2 packs spaghetti noodles (7 ounce size)
2 cans of cream (Media Crema, or use $1^1/2$ cups fresh cream)
1 large can of evaporated milk
1 cup (2 sticks) butter
fresh parsley sprig
salt to taste

Preparation

• Cook spaghetti in $^1/2$ gallon boiling water for 10 minutes
• Drain (do not rinse) and set aside
• Mix cream, milk, butter, and salt in medium-sized pot
• Add spaghetti and parsley
• Stir until creamy and serve

Serves 6

Note
This recipe is quick, easy and delicious, one bite is not enough!

Cho-cho With Spaghetti
and Cilantro

by Sanny's Grill, San Ignacio, Cayo

Ingredients

2 packs spaghetti (7ounce size)
2 large peeled cho-chos, cut into 1/4 inch strips
8 tablespoons butter
8 cloves of garlic, chopped
2 small onions, chopped
1/2 cup dry white wine
2 small carrots, chopped
4 large ripe tomatoes
2 tablespoons lime juice
1/2 cup cilantro, chopped
salt and pepper to taste
grated cheese

Preparation

• Heat butter in skillet
• Add garlic and onions and sauté for a few seconds
• Add cho-cho and sauté for two minutes
• Add wine and stir constantly until wine has evaporated
• Add carrots, tomatoes, lime juice, and cilantro
• Simmer for three minutes then add salt and black pepper
• Put spaghetti on plates and pour cho-cho mixture over it
• Top with grated cheese

Serves 4

stuffed chayote

by duPlooy's Restaurant, Cayo

Ingredients

4 chayote (eggplant or
 zucchini can also be used)
1 packet Protemas (meat substitute)
6 tablespoons olive oil
3 cloves garlic, minced
1 onion, chopped
1 green pepper
3 cups cooked rice
1 teaspoon chili powder
1/2 teaspoon cumin
salt and pepper to taste

Toppings

cheddar or mozzarella cheese
fresh parsley or cilantro
queso blanco

Preparation

• Peel chayote and cut in half lengthwise
• Boil water and add chayote and cook for about 5 minutes, until soft but not soggy
• Immediately remove from hot water and rinse with cold water
• The vegetable should still keep its shape when put on a plate
• Scoop out a hollow in center for filling
• Soak Protemas in water for about 10 minutes
• Drain and squeeze out excess water
• Sauté olive oil, garlic, onion and green pepper
• When soft add spices, drained Protemas and cooked rice and mix together
• Spoon mixture into cooked chayote
• When ready to serve top with grated cheddar or mozzarella cheese and chopped
   fresh parsley or cilantro
• Broil for 5 minutes until cheese is melted and brown
• Garnish with fresh chopped herbs or crumbled queso blanco

Serves 4

Stuffed Green Pepper

by Theo Cocchi, Parrot Nest Lodge, Bullet Tree Falls, Cayo

Ingredients

4 large green, red or yellow peppers, whole
2 onions, diced
2 carrots, diced
1 green pepper, diced
any other vegetables or meat you wish to include in the stuffing
1 tablespoon butter or margarine
1 tablespoon olive oil
a pinch of seasoning salt, pepper, parsley and oregano
1/2 cup cheese
1/4 cup bread crumbs
Parmesan cheese

Preparation

• In a pan boil the peppers whole until tender but not too soft
• Remove from water, cut off the tops and remove seeds
• Place in a baking dish with a bit of water in the bottom to avoid sticking while baking
• Sauté vegetables in a pan with butter, oil and seasonings
• When tender add cheese and bread crumbs
• Fill the peppers with the mixture (you can fill them whole or cut in half lengthwise)
• Sprinkle with more bread crumbs and Parmesan cheese
• Bake for 10-15 minutes at 350°F (177°C)

Serves 4 to 8

Hunkar Begendi
(Grilled Eggplant with Cheese)

by Ahmet Arslan, Princess Hotel and Casino, Belize City

Ingredients

2 large eggplants
$1/2$ lemon
1 cup water
$1/4$ cup butter
1 tablespoon flour
1 cup milk
$1/4$ cup mozzarella cheese, shredded
nutmeg
salt

Preparation

- Smoke whole eggplants in covered barbecue, or roast over the stove's flame, or bake at 350°F (177°C) for 20 to 30 minutes, until tender
- Squeeze the half lemon into a shallow dish of water
- Place eggplants in water, turn to coat thoroughly, and let stand until cool
- Peel eggplants, remove seeds and cut into $1/4$" cubes
- Melt butter in skillet, add flour and cook and stir until light brown
- Stir in milk, add cheese, eggplant, a dash of nutmeg and season to taste with salt
- Cook over very low heat for 5 minutes

Serves 8

Broiled Polenta
With Portobello Mushrooms

by duPlooy's Restaurant, Cayo

Ingredients

5 cups water
3/4 teaspoon salt
1 1/2 cups cornmeal
1/2 cup mozzarella
1/2 cup cheddar cheese
black pepper to taste
2 teaspoons butter
2 tomatoes, thinly sliced in rounds
8 basil leaves
3 tablespoons olive oil
1/2 onion
1 1/2 cups portobello mushrooms, sliced thick
1 large garlic clove
1 tablespoon water or white wine

Note
You can order Portobello mushrooms from Doug Fox in Belize City, but you can also top with sautéed spinach and onions or chaya and onions or canned mushrooms.

Preparation

• Bring water and 1/2 teaspoon salt to a boil
• When boiling add cornmeal in a steady stream while whisking constantly
• Lower heat and simmer until thick (this is the polenta)
• Spread into buttered pan and sprinkle with cheeses and pepper then set aside
• Sauté butter, tomato slices and basil leaves
• Place neatly over cheese and polenta and sprinkle with black pepper
• Sauté onion, mushrooms and garlic in olive oil
• Add water or white wine and 1/4 teaspoon salt
• Spread evenly over tomatoes
• Broil polenta 5-8 minutes before serving

Serves 6

Baked Sweet Potato

by Pooks Hill Kitchen, Roaring River, Cayo

Ingredients

2-3 lbs. sweet potato
1/2 cup melted butter
spring onions (green onions)
salt and pepper

Preparation

- Peel sweet potatoes and cut into 3" chunks
- Cook in salted water for about 5 minutes then drain
- When cold, grate into buttered pie dish
- Layer with butter and spring onions, salt and pepper
- Press firmly
- Cook in oven at 400°F (204°C) until brown, about 45 minutes

Serves 8

Stewed Pumpkin With
Ground Sesame Seeds

by Masanori Kondo, Cayo Centre for Employment Training, San Ignacio

Ingredients

2 lbs. pumpkin
6 tablespoons sesame seeds
2 tablespoons soy sauce (light)
1 tablespoon orange juice
1 tablespoon sugar

Preparation

- Cut pumpkin into big pieces and remove pumpkin seeds
- Remove skin if desired and trim corners
- Boil the pumpkin for 10 minutes
- Roast sesame seeds over low flame until golden and fragrant, being careful not to burn them
- Grind the sesame seeds well
- Put $1^1/2$ cups water, soy sauce, orange juice and sugar in a pan and boil
- Stew pumpkin in the pan over low flame until the pumpkin becomes soft
- Add the ground sesame seeds to the pan and turn off the heat
- Let the pumpkin sit for 20 minutes before serving

Serves 4

Green Papaya Casserole

by Fido's Courtyard & Pier, San Pedro, Ambergris Caye

Ingredients

1 green papaya, (about 2 lbs.) peeled, de-seeded, medium diced
3 large onions, small diced
3 large tomatoes, medium diced
3 garlic cloves, finely chopped
bread crumbs

Preparation:

• Pre-heat oven to 325°F (163°C)
• Sauté the green papaya, onion, garlic and tomatoes in olive oil for about 5 minutes
• Season with salt and pepper to taste
• Place in a casserole dish
• Liberally sprinkle the top with the bread crumbs
• Place in oven and bake for about 30 minutes
• Serve while still hot, spoon onto plates and enjoy!

Serves 4 to 6

Spinach Cakes

by Felicia Nuñez from her book, Gifts From My Heart and My Firehearth

Ingredients

6 ounces fresh spinach
1 egg
1 tablespoon onion, chopped
2 tablespoons margarine or butter
$1/2$ teaspoon salt
$1/2$ teaspoon pepper
$1/2$ cup flour
1 teaspoon baking powder
$1/2$ cup milk
oil for deep frying

Preparation

• Wash spinach and shred finely with a knife
• Add beaten egg, onion, melted margarine
• Stir in dry ingredients
• Add milk to make a very thick batter
• Drop spoonfuls of batter into hot oil and cook until golden brown
• Drain and serve

Serves 4

Curried Green Bananas

by Felicia Nuñez from her book, Gifts From My Heart and My Firehearth

Ingredients

8 green bananas
1 cup coconut milk
1/2 teaspoon hot sauce
1 beaten egg
2 tablespoons curry powder
1 tablespoon butter or margarine
1/2 teaspoon salt
4 servings of boiled rice

Preparation

• Fry curry in butter for 2 minutes
• Peel and slice bananas
• Place in curry mixture and brown slightly
• Add pepper, salt and coconut milk and simmer gently for half an hour
• Stir in beaten egg
• Serve with boiled rice

Serves 4

Tamalitos/Dukunu

by Ilda Garcia, Ilda's Catering, San Ignacio, Cayo

Ingredients

50 ears of green corn with husks
1/2 lb. (1 cup) butter, melted
1-2 tablespoons salt (to taste)
1 tablespoon sugar
1 lb. (2 cups) lard, melted

Preparation

• Husk the corn, cut off the kernels and grind them in a grinder or food processor
• Add the rest of the ingredients and mix well
• Place a large spoonful of the mixture on a corn husk
• Fold the edges of the husk to wrap the mixture
• Place tamalito, fold-side down, on anther husk and repeat folding
• Continue until all the tamalitos are wrapped
• Work quickly or the tamalitos will become bitter
• Place corn cobs in the bottom of a large pot
• Add a second layer of cobs and fill with water to reach the top of the cobs
• Stand the tamalitos on end on top of the corn cobs, cover with more husks and a tight lid
• Steam over a low flame until cooked, about 1/2 hour

Makes 50 tamalitos

Note
Tamalitos, also called dukunu, are often made for special occasions like birthdays or parties. If you're not feeding a crowd you can reduce the ingredients by half.

Jennie's Mexican Rice

by Jennie Staines, Caliente! San Pedro, Ambergris Caye

Ingredients

4 cups rice
1 lb. tomatoes, cooked and peeled
1/4 cup cilantro
1 cup onion, chopped
1/4 cup sweet pepper, chopped
1/2 cup whole corn
1/2 cup carrots, diced
2 tablespoons tomato sauce
1/2 of a small habanero (no seeds)
2 tablespoons vegetable shortening
2 tablespoons butter
2 tablespoons consommé powder or chicken bouillon
salt and black pepper to taste

Preparation

• Peel tomatoes, chop and put in blender
• Add cilantro, 1/2 cup of onion, tomato sauce and habanero
• Purée, adding water to mixture to make 4 1/4 cups liquid
• In a pan add shortening, butter, 1/2 cup of onion, sweet pepper, corn and carrots
• Cook until tender
• Add washed rice, chicken bouillon, salt & pepper to taste
• Add tomato mixture and cook until rice is done

Serves 4 to 6

Jalapeño Rice

by Upstairs Pollito Dorado, San Ignacio, Cayo

Ingredients

2 1/2 cups (1 lb.) rice
1/4 lb. vermicelli
1/2 cup butter
1 jalapeño pepper
1 carrot
1/2 onion
1/2 sweet pepper
1 teaspoon fresh ginger (or dash ginger powder)
2 cloves garlic
salt, pepper and cumin to taste

Preparation

• Fry uncooked vermicelli in 1/2 cup butter until golden brown
• Sprinkle with black pepper and cumin
• Add sliced jalapeños, onions and chopped sweet pepper
• When fried, mix in rice
• Grate carrot and add with minced garlic and ginger
• Add 2 cups water
• Cover and cook over low heat until done, about 45 minutes

Serves 2 to 4

Main Dishes

From the Land

Norwegian Beef Salad

by Ahmet Arslan, Princess Hotel and Casino, Belize City

Ingredients

1 cup cooked beef, veal or lamb, cut into julienne strips
1 cup baked or boiled ham, cut into julienne strips
1 tablespoon onion, minced
6 tablespoons salad oil
2 tablespoons cider vinegar
$1/2$ teaspoon pepper
1 teaspoon parsley, minced
$1/4$ cup heavy cream or sour cream
1 hard boiled egg, sliced
1 boiled or pickled beet, sliced

Preparation

• Mix cut meats with onion
• Beat together oil, vinegar, pepper and parsley
• Stir cream into dressing and mix with meats combining lightly
• Garnish with sliced egg and beet

Serves 4

Pork with Chipotle Honey Glaze

by Robert Argue, Chaa Creek Cottages, Cayo

Ingredients

6 chipotle chilies in adobo ($1/2$ cup)
6 garlic cloves, coarsely chopped
6 tablespoons honey
2 pork chops or pork loin

Preparation:

• Purée chipotle chilies with garlic and honey in a blender until smooth
• Pat pork dry and season with salt
• Place pork on baking sheet and spread with chilies, glaze to coat well
• Roast in middle of oven for 15 - 20 minutes

Serves 2

Sanny's Pork Chops

by Sanny's Grill, San Ignacio, Cayo

Ingredients

1 lb. pork chops, trimmed
2 teaspoons vegetable oil
3 cloves garlic, chopped
1 large onion, sliced
1/4 cup dry white wine
1/4 cup Worcestershire sauce
1 teaspoon honey
salt and pepper to taste
2 tablespoons cornstarch mixed with 1/2 cup water

Preparation

• Lightly season the pork chops with salt and pepper
• Heat frying pan with oil, then add garlic and cook for a few seconds
• Add pork chops until almost cooked
• Add onion and cook for a few seconds
• Add wine and cook for a minute until reduced, shaking the pan over high heat
• Add Worcestershire sauce, honey, salt and black pepper
• Add cornstarch mixture and cook until sauce thickens as desired
• Serve and enjoy!

Serves 2

Ginger Pork

by Masanori Kondo, Cayo Centre for Employment Training, San Ignacio

Ingredients

1 lb. pork loin
2 tablespoons fresh ginger, grated
2 cloves garlic, finely chopped
1/2 onion, sliced
4 tablespoons rum
6 tablespoons soy sauce (light)
2 tablespoons sugar
2 tablespoons orange juice
2 tablespoons sesame oil (or vegetable oil)
1/2 cabbage

Preparation

- Slice onion and pork
- Mix rum, soy sauce, sugar, orange juice, ginger and garlic in a bowl
- Marinate sliced pork and onion in the seasoning liquid for 30 minutes
- Slice cabbage into fine strips and soak them in icy cold water to crisp
- Heat oil in a frying pan and fry the pork and onion
- Add the seasoning liquid to the pan and simmer
- Drain the cabbage well and serve with the pork

Serves 4

Rice and Beans
With Coconut Milk

by Elvi's Kitchen, San Pedro, Ambergris Caye

Ingredients

1 cup red kidney beans
5 cups of water
2 tablespoons onion, chopped
1 garlic clove
salt and pepper
pinch of thyme
2 cups rice
1 cup coconut milk (see recipe)

Coconut Milk:
1 coconut, finely grated
3/4 cup warm water
• Mix the grated coconut and warm water
• Squeeze and strain the mixture to extract milk

Preparation

• Cook beans in pressure cooker until tender (don't add salt until beans are cooked)
• Sauté chopped onion and add to the beans with salt, pepper and a pinch of thyme
• Add the washed rice and coconut milk to the beans
• Cook over low fire, stirring gently from time to time, until rice is cooked
• Serve with your favourite meat, fish or poultry dish

Serves 4

stewed chicken

by Elvi's Kitchen, San Pedro, Ambergris Caye

Ingredients

1 chicken
3 tablespoons oil
3 garlic cloves
pinch of cumin
recado to taste
salt and pepper
1 small sweet pepper
1 tomato
1 small onion

Preparation

• Cut the chicken in pieces and season with salt, pepper, garlic, cumin and recado
• Let chicken season for half an hour
• Fry the chicken pieces in very hot oil until brown
• Add the liquid from the seasoning, sweet pepper, tomato and onion
• Cover and cook over a low flame until tender
• Sprinkle with Worcestershire sauce

Serves 4 to 6

Fried Chicken
with Onion Sauce

by Masanori Kondo, Cayo Centre for Employment Training, San Ignacio

Ingredients

2 lbs. chicken legs
cornstarch for coating

Seasoning for chicken:
2 tablespoons rice wine
2 tablespoons soy sauce
1 pinch black pepper

Onion Sauce:
2 large onions
1 red (hot) pepper
1¼ cups (light) soy sauce
2 tablespoons rum
2 tablespoons vinegar
4 tablespoons sugar

Preparation

• Cut chicken legs in half and sprinkle with seasoning ingredients
• Dice onion and red pepper and fry until fragrant
• Add soy sauce, rice wine, vinegar and sugar to the pan and boil for 3 minutes
• Drain the chicken and sprinkle with cornstarch
• Deep fry chicken in hot oil, at 350°F (177°C), until cooked
• Place the chicken on a serving plate
• Pour the onion sauce over the chicken and serve immediately

Serves 4

Cashew Chicken

by Pamella Picon, Mopan River Resort, Benque Viejo, Cayo

Ingredients

2 lbs. boneless chicken breasts, skinned, diced into 3/4" pieces and drained

2/3 cup whole unsalted cashews, lightly toasted

20 whole dried red chilies

2/3 cup sliced bamboo shoots, cut in 1/2 inch lengths

1 tablespoon fresh ginger, minced

1 tablespoon garlic, minced

3 tablespoons peanut oil

1 tablespoon cilantro, chopped

Sauce:

1/2 cup chicken broth

1/4 cup soy sauce

3 tablespoons dry sherry (or Chinese rice wine)

3 tablespoons oyster sauce

1 1/2 tablespoons rice vinegar

1 1/2 tablespoons white sugar

1/2 teaspoon red pepper flakes

1 tablespoon cornstarch

Preparation

• Combine sauce ingredients and set aside
• Heat oil in a wok, and fry chilies until slightly dark and crisp (don't let them scorch!)
• Remove to drain on a paper towel
• Add garlic and ginger to hot oil, stir fry for 1-2 minutes
• Add chicken and stir fry quickly to coat with oil
• Continue frying until white
• Stir sauce mixture and add to wok along with bamboo shoots
• Stir well to coat meat and allow to thicken slightly
• Turn off heat, and stir in cashews
• Remove to serving dish, and garnish with fried chilies and chopped cilantro

Serves 6

Chicken Pibil

by Mrs. Dahlia Castillo, Tony's Inn & Beach Resort, Corozal Town

Ingredients

1 whole chicken (4 lbs.)
plantain leaves
4 ounces red recado
4 tablespoons ground oregano
2 tablespoons consommé (powder)
5 cloves garlic
1 onion, diced
1 cup water
4 tablespoons vinegar

Preparation

• Wash and cut chicken in half
• Line inside of skillet with plantain leaves
• Place chicken on leaves
• Place recado and all other ingredients in blender
• Blend until a smooth paste is formed and all condiments are properly dissolved
• Pour over chicken and baste well, then cover with additional plantain leaves
• Cover skillet and cook at a very low temperature for 1-2 hours

Serves 8

Note
Pibil is a Yucatec Maya dish, traditionally cooked in an a pit lined with hot stones and coals. Chicken must be well basted in sauce before cooking and slow cooking is a must as it allows ingredients to blend and enhance flavors.

to Serve Chicken Pibil

Chicken Pibil can be served in the following ways:

Soft Tacos: Fill corn tortillas with shredded chicken, roll and moisten with some gravy.

Chicken Tostadas: Deep fry corn tortillas until crisp, top with refried beans, shredded chicken, cheese, lettuce and diced tomatoes, sour cream optional.

Chicken Burritos: Place refried beans and shredded chicken on flour tortillas and roll.

Serve with **Pico de Gallo:**
Diced tomatoes, onions, cilantro, salt & pepper to taste, lime juice & dash olive oil.

Macy's Curry Chicken

by Macy's Cafe, Belize City and San Ignacio

Ingredients

1 whole chicken (3 lbs.)
1 tablespoon black pepper
1 tablespoon garlic powder
3 tablespoons curry powder
3 tablespoons oil
4 potatoes, peeled and quartered
1 onion, sliced in rings
1 sweet pepper, chopped
salt to taste

Preparation

• Wash chicken with lime and water and cut chicken into small pieces
• Add salt, black pepper, garlic and curry powder to season chicken
• Add 8 cups of water
• Heat oil in a pot, when hot add the chicken
• Cook for 20 minutes
• Add potatoes, onion, sweet pepper to pot and cook for next 20 minutes
• Serve with white rice or rice and beans and a side of green salad

Serves 4 to 5

Escabeche

by Fido's Courtyard & Pier, San Pedro, Ambergris Caye

Ingredients

1 whole chicken, cut in quarters
$1/2$ gallon of water
$1/2$ cup of white wine vinegar
small handful of allspice seed
2 lbs. onions, cut in rings
1 tablespoon dried oregano

Preparation

• In a large sauté pan fry chicken in cooking oil
• Drain oil and set chicken aside
• In a large stockpot bring water, allspice, and oregano to a boil
• Add the onions
• Cook for about 5-10 minutes, or until onions become translucent
• Add the chicken
• To serve place chicken in a deep bowls, spoon in onions and fill with broth

Serves 6

Yogurt Ginger Chicken

by Fido's Courtyard & Pier, San Pedro, Ambergris Caye

Ingredients

6 chicken breasts
4 cloves garlic
2 tablespoons fresh ginger, grated
1 cup yogurt

Preparation

- Score chicken, making a few shallow cuts along its length
- Place in ceramic or glass bowl (not metal as it will react with the marinade)
- In a blender, blend garlic, ginger and yogurt
- Pour into bowl over chicken
- Marinate at least 4-6 hours or overnight, no longer
- Remove chicken from marinade and place in sealed container and refrigerate
- Place in a pan and bake at 375°F (191°C) or until golden brown

Serves 6

Roman Chicken

by Masanori Kondo, Cayo Centre for Employment Training, San Ignacio

Ingredients

1^1/2 lbs. chicken
1 large onion
1 green pepper
3 cloves garlic
2 anchovies (or sardines)
^{1}/4 cup white wine
^{1}/4 cup olive oil
1 tomato
2 cups tomato sauce
^{1}/2 cup water
flour for coating
salt and black pepper

Preparation

- Cut chicken into big pieces and season with salt and black pepper
- Cut onion and green pepper into round slices
- Cut tomato into cubes and mash garlic
- Cut anchovies into fine pieces
- Sprinkle flour over the chicken
- Brown chicken in hot oil in frying pan and set aside
- Heat olive oil in heavy saucepan and fry garlic until fragrant
- Add onion, green pepper and anchovies to the saucepan
- Add the chicken, white wine, tomato, tomato sauce and water and bring to a boil
- Lower heat and cook gently for 30 minutes
- Add salt and black pepper to taste

Serves 4

Stewed Beef

by Fido's Courtyard & Pier, San Pedro, Ambergris Caye

Ingredients

1¹/2 lbs. beef
¹/2 gallon of water
2 ounces recado
1 bell pepper, sliced
1 medium onion, sliced
2 tomatoes, chopped
2 tablespoons Worcestershire sauce

Preparation

• Heat oil in a large sauté pan and fry the meat
• Drain oil and set beef aside
• In another large pot bring the water to a boil
• Add recado, mix well
• Add onion, bell pepper and tomato
• Bring the mixture down to a simmer and add the beef
• Season with salt and pepper
• Let simmer for about 20 minutes
• Serve with rice and beans and fried plantain

Serves 6

Spiced Beef Tenderloin with Mango Salsa

by Kenrick Theus, Lamanai Outpost Lodge, Indian Church, Orange Walk

Ingredients

12 - 4 ounce beef tenderloin steaks
olive oil

Spice Mix:
1 tablespoon ground cinnamon
1 tablespoon ground coriander
1 tablespoon salt
1 tablespoon paprika
1^1/2 teaspoons salt
^{1}/2 teaspoon cayenne pepper

Salsa:
^{1}/4 cup jalapeños, diced
^{1}/4 cup mixed fruit jam (try Melindas!)
2^1/2 cups mangoes, peeled, pitted
    and diced
1^1/4 cups red bell peppers, chopped
^{3}/4 cup red onion, chopped
^{1}/3 cup cilantro, chopped

Preparation

• Mix all ingredients for salsa together
• Season to taste with salt and pepper and chill
• Combine all the spice ingredients and mix well
• Brush steak with olive oil and sprinkle ^{1}/2 teaspoon of spice mix over each side of steak
• Prepare grill at medium high heat
• Cook for about 2-3 minutes on each side for medium rare to medium
• Serve with salsa on the side for a truly tropical and refreshing meal!

Serves 6

Chorizo and Egg Burritos

by Mrs. Dahlia Castillo, Tony's Inn & Beach Resort, Corozal Town

Ingredients

3 - 1oz. breakfast sausages or chorizo
1/4 onion, diced small
sprig cilantro, chopped
4 eggs
dash salt
dash pepper
3 slices cheese
4 flour tortillas
Refried beans
Salsa (prepared or use recipe at right)

Preparation

• Crumble sausage and cook in hot saucepan, remove from heat and set aside
• Sauté onions, add beaten eggs with cilantro
• Add salt and pepper to taste
• Top eggs with melted cheese
• Fill each flour tortilla with beans, sausage, eggs and melted cheese
• Serve with salsa

Serves 4

Salsa:
3 tomatoes, diced
1/2 onion chopped
1 sprig cilantro, chopped
1/2 tablespoon Marie Sharp's pepper sauce
1/2 cup lime juice, freshly squeezed
salt and freshly ground pepper to taste

Combine the tomatoes, onion, cilantro and pepper sauce in a bowl. Add lime juice gradually, to give it a sour taste. Add salt and pepper to taste.

Black Bean Combo

by Jennie Staines, Caliente!, San Pedro, Ambergris Caye

Ingredients

1 1/2 cups black beans, cooked with 1 clove garlic and 1/2 onion
1/4 cup vegetable shortening
1/4 cup bacon, chopped
1 cup polish sausage, sliced
1 cup smoked ham, diced
1/4 cup cilantro, chopped
1/2 cup onions, chopped
1/2 cup sweet pepper, chopped
1 clove garlic, crushed
1/2 cup fresh tomatoes, peeled
1/2 cup carrots, diced
1/2 cup potatoes, diced
2 beef bouillon cubes
2 tablespoons Mrs. Elvie's (or another) hot sauce
salt and pepper to taste

Preparation

- To cook the black beans wash them thoroughly and place in 10 cups water
- Add 1 clove minced garlic and half of large chopped onion, and cook until beans are soft adding more water if needed
- In another large saucepan, add shortening and bacon and cook until bacon is crispy
- Add onions, sweet peppers, garlic, cilantro, tomatoes, carrots, potato, sausage and ham and cook for 3 minutes
- Add beans and all seasonings
- Cook for 1 1/2 hours stirring frequently
- Serve with corn or flour tortillas

Serves 6 to 8

Note
Cook the beans the day before for better results.

Meatballs Wrapped
in Cabbage Leaves

by Masanori Kondo, Cayo Centre for Employment Training, San Ignacio

Ingredients

8 whole cabbage leaves
1 onion, sliced
1/2 carrot, sliced
3 cups consommé soup (or use 3 cups
   water with powdered soup concentrate)
salt and black pepper
1 medium can tomato sauce

Filling:
1 cup ground meat
2 1/2 tablespoons onion
2 tablespoons green pepper
1 egg yolk
salt and black pepper

Preparation

- For filling, finely chop onion and green pepper and fry until tender, then cool
- In a bowl combine ground meat, fried onion and green pepper, egg yolk, salt and black pepper and mix well
- Divide meat mixture into 8 meatballs and shape into cylinders
- Parboil cabbage leaves for 3 minutes
- Drain the cabbage, remove the hard center and sprinkle lightly with salt and black pepper
- Wrap the meat in the cabbage leaf and pin the edge with a toothpick
- Boil consommé in a pot and add sliced onion and sliced carrot
- Boil the rolled cabbage in the consommé for 20 minutes over a low flame
- Add tomato sauce to the pot and boil 5-10 minutes over a low flame
- Season with salt and black pepper and serve

Serves 4

Breadfruit Meat or Fish Rolls

by Felicia Nuñez from her book Gifts From My Heart and My Firehearth

Ingredients

1 medium breadfruit
1 lb. cooked, flaked fish or ground meat
1 medium sweet pepper, chopped
2 teaspoons thyme
4 basil leaves
3 tablespoons butter or margarine
2 teaspoons lime juice
1 egg

Preparation

• Wash and cut breadfruit into 8 slices, peel and core
• Put into boiling, salted water and cook just until soft
• Chop basil finely and sauté in 1 tablespoon butter with thyme and sweet pepper
• Add fish or meat and remove from flame
• Mash breadfruit, then stir in egg, lime juice and 2 tablespoons butter
• Form into a smooth dough and let stand 5 minutes
• Roll dough into balls then pat out into flat circles (as for panades)
• Place a spoonful of meat/fish mixture in center of dough and fold in half to cover
• Pinch edges to seal and place in a greased baking pan
• Brush with a little butter
• Bake at 350°F (177°C) until brown

Serves 4 to 6

Note
Vegetarians can use cheese or scrambled eggs instead of fish or meat.

Spicy Mango Curry Sauce

by Chef Maurice, Wish Willy Bar and Grill

Ingredients

2 mangoes, diced
1 small onion, diced
1 tablespoon curry powder
pinch of coriander and cumin to taste
salt, pepper and chili pepper

Preparation

• Cook mango, curry, cumin, coriander, salt and pepper for 10 minutes
• Add chili pepper
• Serve over cooked fish, lobster or chicken

Serves 4

Orange Balsamic Sauce

by Robert Argue, Chaa Creek Cottages, Cayo

Ingredients

1 medium red onion
1 cup orange juice
$1/2$ cup balsamic vinegar
1-2 tablespoons sugar

Preparation:

• Halve onion through root end and cut crosswise into very thin slices
• In a saucepan simmer onion with the orange juice and vinegar, stirring occasionally until liquid is reduced and thickened, 30 - 40 minutes
• Stir in sugar and salt to taste and cook mixture over low heat, stirring until sugar is dissolved
• Serve sauce warm over baked fish or chicken

Yields about one cup.

Main Dishes

From the Sea

Snapper Caribe

by Chef Sean Beaton, Catering by Design, Gales Point Manatee

Ingredients

1 lb. snapper fillet (or any
white firm-fleshed fish)
1/4 cup sweet pepper
1/4 cup onion
1/4 cup tomato
1/4 cup carrots
1/4 cup zucchini or cucumber
2 teaspoons ketchup
1 teaspoon brown sugar
1 teaspoon hot pepper sauce or to taste
(preferably habanero pepper sauce)

1/4 cup water
1/4 cup butter
3 teaspoons cooking oil
salt and pepper
1 teaspoon oregano
1 teaspoon thyme

Preparation

- Chop the vegetable ingredients into large mince and sauté with butter until tender
- Add thyme, oregano, brown sugar, ketchup and pepper sauce
- Simmer for 5 minutes with water
- In another frying pan heat cooking oil on medium high heat
- Season fillet with salt and pepper and sear fillet in pan
- Cook until the edges brown slightly, turn fillet over only once and sear fillet until flaky (not dry)
- Place fillet on a plate, pour salsa (recipes on pages 24 and 84) over fillet and serve

Serves 2

Note
This dish is also great to BBQ and should be served with coconut rice or plain white rice.

Seafood Lasagna

by Franco's Restaurant, Luba Hati, Placencia Penninsula

Ingredients

1$^{1}/2$ lbs. dry lasagna noodles
$^{1}/2$ lb. snapper fillet, cut in small pieces
$^{1}/2$ lb. lobster meat, cut up and parboiled
$^{1}/2$ lb. small shrimp, peeled and deveined
$^{1}/4$ lb. crab meat (optional)
$^{1}/2$ lb. conch, ground up with a meat grinder
$^{1}/4$ cup Parmesan cheese
2 $^{1}/2$ quarts béchamel sauce (recipe follows)
$^{1}/4$ teaspoon nutmeg
$^{1}/2$ cup chopped fresh basil leaves and parsley

Preparation

- Partially cook lasagna in large quantity of boiling, salted water
- Drain and cool in ice water while still very much 'al dente'
- Lay out on one half of clean tablecloth
- Cover the lasagna strips until needed with the other half of the cloth
- Prepare the béchamel and season with nutmeg, salt and white pepper
- Reserve two cups of the sauce for the top
- Stir in the fish, lobster, shrimp, conch and crab while the sauce is bubbling hot and remove from heat
- Add the herbs and taste for seasoning
- Butter a baking pan and spread a little of the béchamel on the bottom

- Place one layer of pasta on the bottom of the pan followed by a third of the sauce and fish mixture
- Sprinkle with Parmesan cheese
- Place another layer of pasta at 90 degrees (crosswise) to the first one
- Repeat two more times finishing with the reserved white sauce and plenty of Parmesan cheese
- Dot with butter and bake in preheated 350°F (177°C) oven for 1/2 hour
- Let rest for 15 minutes then cut in squares and serve

Serves 6 to 8

Béchamel Sauce

Ingredients

6 tablespoons butter
6 tablespoons flour
3 quarts (12 cups) of milk
salt and pepper to taste

Preparation

- Melt butter in 4-quart saucepan
- Add flour and cook a few minutes to make very light roux
- Add milk and bring almost to boil while stirring
- Reduce the heat and continue to stir until the sauce thickens

Note
The sauce should not be too thin because the seafood will release a certain amount of fluid.

Fish With cashew Sauce

by José Ortiz, Ramon's Village, San Pedro, Ambergris Caye

Ingredients

8 fish fillets
1 teaspoon salt
1/4 teaspoon freshly ground black pepper
1/4 cup flour
6 tablespoons butter
4 ounces (1/2 cup) cashews
1 teaspoon fresh parsley, finely chopped
1 1/2 teaspoon garlic, finely chopped
1/2 cup finely chopped onions
2 tablespoons fresh lime juice

Preparation

• Wash fish fillet and season with salt and pepper
• Dip in flour, then fry in butter until golden brown
• In another pan fry the cashews with butter
• Mix with the parsley, garlic, onion and lime juice and place it on top of the fillet

Serves 8

Fish Escabeche

by Caladium Restaurant, Belmopan

Ingredients

4 snappers (8-10 ounce size)
2 limes
salt and black pepper for seasoning
vegetable oil for frying
1 lb. onions
1 small sweet pepper
6 medium tomatoes
1/2 stalk celery
cilantro (a few sprigs)
2 tablespoons coconut oil
6 tablespoons tomato paste, dissolved in $1^1/2$ cups water
thyme
hot pepper sauce (optional)

Preparation

- Scale, clean and rub fish with lime
- Score and season with salt and black pepper
- Half fry fish in very hot (but not smoking) vegetable oil - about 3 minutes on each side
- Drain on paper towel and set aside
- Slice onions, sweet pepper, and tomatoes in rings, dice celery, mince cilantro
- Heat coconut oil in large saucepan and stir-fry vegetables
- Add dissolved tomato paste, sprinkle black pepper, thyme, hot sauce and salt to taste
- Bring to a simmer, then lay half-fried fish in sauce, cover and continue to simmer for about 10 minutes
- Serve fish with a slice of lime, rice and beans, fried plantain and garden salad (or a vegetable of your choice)

Serves 4

Spicy Fish Fingers

by Elvi's Kitchen, San Pedro, Ambergris Caye

Ingredients

4 fish fillets
8 tablespoons Marie Sharp's hot pepper sauce
1 egg
2 garlic cloves
salt and pepper
flour for dredging
oil for frying

Preparation

• Cut fish fillet into fingers
• Marinate in garlic, salt, pepper and hot pepper sauce for one hour
• Dry fish
• Dip fish in beaten egg and dredge in flour
• Fry fish in a small amount of hot oil until golden
• Serve with green salad with vinaigrette sauce (see recipe on page 49)

Serves 4

Fish Fillet
in Garlic and Wine

by Elvi's Kitchen, San Pedro, Ambergris Caye

Ingredients

4 fish fillets
4 cloves garlic
salt and pepper
1/4 cup white wine
oil for frying

Preparation

• Cut fillets into square pieces and season with salt and pepper
• Mince garlic and fry in oil until soft
• Pour in white wine, add fish and cover
• Cook over a slow flame until tender

Serves 4

Hudutu Baruru Falumoun
(mashed plantains with sere)

by Felicia Nuñez from her book Gifts From My Heart and My Firehearth

Ingredients

6-7 green plantains
2 coconuts, finely grated
2 lbs. fish, well-seasoned
1 onion
pepper sauce to taste
4 leaves of cilantro
1 teaspoon oregano
1 clove garlic
1/2 teaspoon black pepper

Preparation

• Grate coconut, pour water over it and squeeze milk into a cooking pot to make sere
• Add spices and fish and cook fish until done, stirring constantly so milk does not curdle
• Meanwhile, peel and wash green plantains
• Cook them in water without salt
• When soft and cooled, put into a mortar and pound with foo-foo pounder or mortar stick
• Dip mortar stick in cold water frequently to prevent plantain from sticking
• Pound until plantains hold together and become soft and sticky
• Take out of mortar and serve with fish and coconut milk sere

Serves 4

Shrimp and Feta Pasta

by Chef Whiz, Tranquility Lodge, Jacintoville, Toledo District

Ingredients

4 servings ready-cut noodles or any pasta ou like
48 medium shrimp
4 tablespoons butter
1 cup (more if you like) feta cheese
2 cups fresh tomatoes, chopped
2 cups calaloo, chopped (spinach can be substituted)
dash of white pepper

Preparation

• Cook the noodles according to the directions while you prepare the shrimp and feta
   cheese
• Sauté shrimp in butter, until nearly done
• Add about half of the feta cheese and continue to cook for a minute
• Add half the tomatoes and continue cooking
• Add calaloo and dash of white pepper and cook for just a few minutes more
• Add the rest of the feta cheese and tomatoes and stir
• Remove from heat and serve over drained noodles

Serves 4

Note
*This delicious meal can be prepared in less than 15 minutes! Calaloo grows wild or can
be cultivated very easily. It grows best in areas that have been burned, and gets to 6 feet
tall with leaves that look very much like spinach. You can cook it up as a side vegetable
like any other green.*

Belikin Beer Battered
Coconut Shrimp With Lisette's Secret Sauce

by Chan Chich Lodge, Gallon Jug

Ingredients

1 lb. shrimp
desiccated coconut for coating shrimp
oil for frying

Beer Batter:
1 cup all purpose flour
1 egg
$1/2$ cup (or more) Belikin beer
salt and pepper to taste

Preparation

• Mix all batter ingredients together
• Batter should be slightly thick and have the consistency of pancake batter
• If batter is too thick add more beer until it is the right consistency
• Can be made ahead and refrigerated
• Peel and devein shrimp, leaving tails intact
• Season shrimp with salt and pepper
• Over a medium high flame, heat about $1/2$ inch of oil in frying pan
• Dip shrimp in batter and coat fully
• Roll shrimp in coconut
• Fry shrimp in batches, about 2 minutes per side or until light golden brown
• Serve immediately with Lisette's Secret Sauce, a Gallon Jug product

Serves 4 (if using 36/40 sized shrimp), as an appetizer it can serve up to 10

Note
This makes a fantastic appetizer or main course.

Shrimp and Goat Cheese Tamales

by Jennie Staines, Caliente!, San Pedro, Ambergris Caye

Ingredients

2 lbs. corn masa
3/4 goat cheese, crumbled
1/2 teaspoon salt or to taste
4 tablespoons butter
1/4 cup sweet pepper, minced
2 onions, small, finely chopped
1 clove garlic, minced
1 cup tomatoes, roasted or boiled, peeled and chopped
1/2 lb. shrimp, deveined & chopped

Sauce:
1 tablespoon chile chipotle (adobados)
1 tablespoon butter
2 cups sour cream
salt and freshly ground pepper corns

Melt butter over low heat, add chilies (puréed in blender) and sour cream
Stir until mixture is bubbly, add salt and pepper to taste, stir well

Preparation

- In a saucepan melt butter and cook garlic, onions, sweet pepper and tomatoes until tender
- Add shrimp, salt and pepper to taste
- Knead the masa with goat cheese and salt until uniform in texture
- Divide the dough into balls
- Flatten balls until 1/8 inch thick on a banana leaf or foil (should cover 2"x 4" area)
- Place a spoonful of the shrimp mixture in the center of flattened masa
- Wrap with the banana leaf to form a little package
- Steam for about 45 to 55 minutes, masa separates easily from leaf or foil when opened
- Unwrap and pour sauce over tamales to serve

Serves 4

Celi's Stone Crab Stuffing

by San Pedro Holiday Hotel, Ambergris Caye

Ingredients

1 cup celery, chopped
1 cup onions, chopped
1 cup green peppers, chopped
1/2 cup sliced canned mushrooms
2 cups stone crab meat, cooked and shredded
1 loaf white bread, cubed
1/2 cup (1 stick) butter

Dressing:
1 tablespoon mayonnaise
1 tablespoon mustard
2 eggs, well beaten
1/4 teaspoon garlic
1/2 teaspoon salt
1/2 teaspoon pepper

Preparation

- In large saucepan, over medium heat, melt butter and sauté celery, onion and green pepper until tender, do not overcook
- In a large bowl, combine bread, mushrooms, sautéed vegetables, crabmeat, and dressing ingredients and mix well
- Put mixture into a rectangular baking dish, cover, and bake at 350°F (177°C) for 45 minutes
- Uncover and bake an additional 15 minutes

Serves 8

Note
This recipe was invented to complement Celi's Restaurant's Caribbean Thanksgiving dinner. Stone crab stuffing has become a yearly Thanksgiving and Christmas tradition.

Absolut Citron Lobster
With Roasted Red Pepper Linguine

by Chef Sean Beaton, Catering by Design, Gales Point Manatee

Ingredients

1¹/2 lbs. lobster (cold water lobster can be used as well as spiny lobster)
2 teaspoons butter
1 shot (1 ounce) Absolut Citron vodka
1/4 cup orange juice
2 cloves garlic
2 teaspoons Italian seasoning
1 red pepper, roasted*
1/2 lb. linguine noodles, cooked
2 teaspoons olive oil

Preparation

- Roast pepper by charring over gas flame on stove top or roast in oven for 20 minutes at 400°F (204°C). Wrap in a wet paper towel until cool, then remove charred skin.
- Remove lobster from shell by splitting the shell along the back of the tail with a sharp knife
- Remove and dice meat
- Heat a sauté pan over medium-high heat
- Add butter and lobster, sauté delicately adding garlic and Italian season
- Add vodka, flambé taking pan away from fire and use a lighter or match to carefully ignite
- Return to stove and simmer with orange juice
- In a separate sauté pan add oil, red pepper and cooked linguine and sauté until hot
- Serve lobster sauté over linguine

Serves 4

Desserts

Island Crème Brûlée

by G. Schwendinger, Rendezvous Restaurant and Winery, North Ambergris Caye

Ingredients

4 whole eggs
8 egg yolks
2 cups milk
2 cups cream (35 percent)
2 cups sugar
1 teaspoon vanilla

Preparation

- Mix eggs, milk, sugar and cream until smooth then add vanilla
- Pour mixture into ramekins and bake in oven at 300°F (149°C) for approximately one hour or until set
- Note that ramekins must be placed on a baking sheet with 3/4" of water so mixture will not boil
- When done let cool
- Sprinkle surface with sugar and use a blowtorch or place under a broiler to caramelize sugar
- Cool crust and serve

Serves 6 to 8

Caramel Nut Banana

by Sanny's Grill, San Ignacio, Cayo

Ingredients

3 ripe bananas
1 tablespoon butter
1 tablespoon brown sugar
$1/4$ cup brandy
$1/4$ cup whipping cream
dash of cinnamon
$1/4$ cup peanuts

Preparation

• Heat the butter in a skillet, cook sugar until lightly brown
• Add bananas for a minute, then turn bananas on other side for another minute
• Pour brandy and ignite, then add cream and cinnamon until caramelized
• Serve immediately topped with nuts

Serves 3

Banana in Custard Sauce

by Five Sisters Lodge, Cayo

Ingredients

3 teaspoons sugar
2 tablespoons cornstarch
1/2 cup water
8 ounces cream cheese
1/2 tin condensed milk
juice of 1 large lime
4 teaspoons honey
2 bananas (per serving)
cherries and cherry sauce to decorate

Preparation

• Mix cornstarch and sugar in water, stir while bringing to a boil and cook until thick
• In a blender, combine all remaining ingredients except for the bananas and cherries
• Begin blending the ingredients on low speed
• Slowly add the cornstarch mixture, one teaspoon at a time
• When everything has been added, blend for one minute on high speed
• Place mixture in container and place in freezer for one hour before serving
• To serve sundae style slice bananas at a slanted angle and place in a medium bowl
• Take one scoop of custard mixture and place on top of sliced bananas
• Decorate with cherry and cherry sauce

Serves 2 to 4

Note
This dessert gets the highest marks from our guests for its rich and creamy taste.

Banana Bread

by Five Sisters Lodge, Cayo

Ingredients

8 ripe bananas
2 cups sugar
4 cups (1 lb.) flour
2 teaspoons baking soda
2 cups milk
1/2 cup vegetable oil
2 large eggs
1 tablespoon vinegar

Preparation

• Mash the bananas in a medium sized bowl, then add sugar and mix
• Combine flour and soda in another bowl
• Blend the milk, oil, eggs and vinegar together and add alternately to banana mixture along with the dry ingredients, mixing after each addition
• Blend for 10 more minutes, then pour it into 2 greased loaf pans
• Bake at 350°F (177°C) for 45 minutes to 1 hour

Makes 2 loaves

Bread Pudding

by Yoli's Pizza & Ice Cream Shoppe, San Ignacio, Cayo

Ingredients

2 loaves bread
$1/2$ cup (1 stick) butter
1 large can evaporated milk
2 cups white sugar
2 tablespoons brown sugar
2 tablespoons vanilla
1 teaspoon white rum
$1/2$ teaspoon cinnamon
$1/2$ teaspoon nutmeg
2 eggs
$1/2$ cup raisins

Preparation

- In a large bowl, soak white bread in fresh water for 5 minutes
- Squeeze the water out of the bread and place it in another bowl
- Mix the bread with melted butter, milk, white sugar and eggs
- Blend with a pastry cutter or potato masher until bread is broken down
- Add vanilla, white rum, cinnamon, raisins and nutmeg and mix with large spoon
- Place batter into a greased 8" pan
- Bake for 45 minutes at 350°F (177°C)
- Cool in pan for at least a half hour before serving

Serves 6

Note
When it is still warm it is delicious served with evaporated milk. Refrigerate any leftovers.

Coconut-Mango Crisp

by Felicia Nuñez from her book Gifts From My Heart and My Firehearth

Ingredients

4 large mangoes, peeled and sliced
$1/2$ cup butter or margarine
$1/3$ cup brown sugar
$1/2$ cup oats
$1/2$ cup grated coconut
$1/4$ cup coconut milk
$1/2$ cup white sugar
1 egg
$1/2$ teaspoon cinnamon
1 teaspoon vanilla
$1/2$ cup flour

Preparation

• Place mango slices in a buttered baking dish
• Sprinkle with white sugar and cinnamon
• Cream brown sugar and butter
• Add egg, vanilla, coconut milk and coconut
• Stir in flour and oats
• Spread batter over mangoes
• Bake at 375°F (191°C) for 35 minutes or until golden

Serves 4 to 6

Sweet Potato in Syrup

by Masanori Kondo, Cayo Centre for Employment Training, San Ignacio

Ingredients

1 lb. sweet potatoes
1 tablespoon roasted sesame seeds

Syrup:
1/2 cup sugar
2 tablespoons water

Preparation

• Peel sweet potato and cut into chunks
• Deep fry sweet potato in hot oil until the edges become light brown
• Remove from hot oil and drain well
• Put syrup ingredients in a pan and boil until light brown
• Mix the sweet potato with the syrup and sprinkle roasted sesame over it
• Spread oil on a plate and set the sweet potato on it to cool and serve

Serves 4

Anin Dofu
(Almond Jelly)

by Masanori Kondo, Cayo Centre for Employment Training, San Ignacio

Ingredients

fresh fruit (any kind desired, cubed)
$1/2$ cup evaporated milk
$1/2$ cup condensed milk

To make gelatin:
$1^2/3$ cups water
1 tablespoon gelatin
2 tablespoons sugar
1 tablespoon almond powder

To make syrup:
2 cups water
$2/3$ cup sugar
1 tablespoon lime juice
almond essence

Preparation

• Mix milk together in a bowl
• Put gelatin mixture in a pan and heat it to melt gelatin
• Add milk to gelatin mixture and bring to boil, then strain into a container
• Add almond powder, cover and refrigerate until it sets
• Mix syrup ingredients together
• Cut fruit into cubes, soak them in $1/3$ of syrup and refrigerate
• Put remaining $2/3$ of syrup in a bowl
• Cut the almond jelly into cubes and place in syrup
• Mix the fruit with the almond jelly

Serves 4

Fruit Cocktail

by Masanori Kondo, Cayo Centre for Employment Training, San Ignacio

Ingredients

fresh fruit, any kind you like
2/3 cup granulated sugar
3 tablespoons lemon juice
2 tablespoons rum

Preparation

• Cut fruit into pieces
• Put fruit and lemon juice in a bowl and sprinkle granulated sugar over it
• Let it sit for 20-30 minutes
• Put it in a refrigerator to chill
• Just before eating, sprinkle rum over the fruit and mix
• Serve it with ice cream if you like

Serves 4

Lokum
(Turkish Delight)

by Ahmet Arslan, Princess Hotel, Belize City

Ingredients

4 cups granulated sugar
4 1/2 cups water
1 teaspoon lemon juice
1 cup cornstarch
1 teaspoon cream of tartar
1 tablespoon rose water (may be doubled)
red food coloring
1/2 cup chopped, toasted almonds
3/4 cup confectioners' sugar
1/4 cup cornstarch

Preparation

- Combine sugar, 1 1/2 cups water and lemon juice in a heavy sauce pan
- Stir over low heat until sugar dissolves, brushing sugar crystals off side of pan with bristle brush dipped in cold water
- Bring to a boil and cook to soft ball stage, 240°F (116°C) on a candy thermometer
- Remove from heat
- In another thick-based pan blend cornstarch, cream of tartar and 1 cup cold water until smooth
- Boil remaining 2 cups water and stir into cornstarch mixture, then place over low heat
- Stir constantly until mixture thickens and bubbles
- Use a whisk if lumps form

- Pour hot syrup gradually into cornstarch mixture, stirring constantly
- Bring to a boil and cook gently for 1 1/4 hours
- Stir occasionally with a wooden spoon and cook until mixture is a pale golden colour, stirring is essential
- Stir in rose water to taste and add a few drops of red food colouring to give it pale pink tinge
- Blend in nuts if used, and remove from heat
- Pour into an oiled 23 cm (9 inch) square cake tin and leave for 12 hours to set
- Combine confectioners' sugar and the 1/4 cup cornstarch in a flat dish
- Cut Turkish Delight into squares with an oiled knife and toss in sugar mixture
- Store in a sealed container with remaining sugar mixture sprinkled between layers

Variations:

Crème de Menthe Lokum
Replace rose water and red food colouring with 2 tablespoons Crème de Menthe liqueur and a little green food colouring. Omit nuts.

Orange Lokum
Use 1-2 tablespoons orange flower water instead of rose water; use orange food colouring.

Vanilla Lokum
Use 2 teaspoons vanilla essence instead of rose water and colouring, stir in 1/2 cup toasted chopped almonds or chopped walnuts. Do not blanch almonds.

Serves 8

Black Cake
(Fruit cake)

by Felicia Nuñez from her book Gifts From My Heart and My Firehearth

Ingredients

8 eggs, beaten
4 cups brown sugar
1 cup brown sugar to stew the fruit
2 cups butter
8 cups flour
1 teaspoon fresh nutmeg, grated
1 teaspoon allspice
2 cups rum for stewing fruit
2 lbs. mixed fruit
1 lb. raisins
1 cup nuts
2 large tins evaporated milk
4 teaspoons baking powder
2 cups blackening (caramel coloring)

Preparation

- In large saucepan, put fruits, 1 cup brown sugar and rum
- Stew for 5 minutes and turn off flame
- In a large bowl, cream sugar and butter together
- Add beaten eggs slowly
- Pour in milk and blackening and mix well
- Add flour, baking powder, nutmeg and allspice gradually
- Add stewed fruits along with stewing liquid to cake batter
- Stir in nuts
- Line cake tins with brown paper and fill to 3/4 full
- Bake at 300°F (149°C) for 3 hours

Serves 6 to 8

Butter Rum Cake

by Felicia Nuñez from her book Gifts From My Heart and My Firehearth

Ingredients

1/4 cup rum
1/4 cup raisins
1 cup butter, soft
1 cup sugar
3 eggs
2 teaspoons baking powder
1/2 teaspoon salt
2 1/4 cups flour

Preparation

- Pour rum over raisins and set aside
- Cream butter until light and fluffy
- Add sugar and eggs slowly, beating after each addition
- Continue beating for 3-5 minutes
- Fold in raisins with rum
- Sift flour, baking powder and salt together, stir them into batter
- Pour into greased and floured baking tin
- Bake at 350°F (177°C) for 35 minutes

Serves 8

Banana or Orange Cake
Made the Easy Way

by Theo Cocchi, Parrot Nest Lodge, Bullet Tree Falls, Cayo

Ingredients

$1/2$ cup butter or margarine
1 cup sugar
2 eggs
1 teaspoon vanilla
2 heaping tablespoons yogurt (any flavour)
3 ripe bananas, mashed
$3/4$ teaspoon baking powder
$3/4$ teaspoon baking soda
2 cups flour

Preparation

• In a large mixing bowl mix the butter and sugar until smooth
• Add and mix vanilla, eggs, yogurt and bananas
• Combine baking powder, baking soda and flour
• Add to other ingredients and mix together
• Pour into a greased cake pan or baking dish and bake at 350°F (177°C) for 30 minutes

Orange-Banana Cake
Use recipe above and mix in 2-3 tablespoons of chunky orange marmalade and increase the flour by $1/3$ cup

Serves 8

Note
You can sprinkle the top of cake with almond or walnut pieces or granola before baking.

Lime Pie

by Theo Cocchi, Parrot Nest Lodge, Bullet Tree Falls, Cayo

Ingredients

Pie Crust:
1 1/3 cups graham cracker crumbs
2 tablespoons sugar
a dash or two cinnamon
5 tablespoons butter or margarine

Filling:
4 large egg yolks
1 tin condensed milk
3/4 cup freshly squeezed lime juice

Topping:
1/2 cup sugar
2 tablespoons water
4 egg whites
1/2 teaspoon cream of tartar

Preparation

- Prepare crust by melting butter, add and mix with dry ingredients and press into pie pan. Bake at 350°F (177°C) for 5 minutes then set aside
- Prepare filling by beating egg yolks in a bowl, by hand or electrix mixer. Mix in condensed milk and slowly pour in lemon juice while beating. Once mixture thickens, set aside
- Prepare topping by stirring sugar and water together in a small pan
- Heat, stirring until bubbling, remove pan from heat and set aside
- In a mixing bowl beat egg whites until foamy
- Add cream of tartar and beat until stiff
- In a steady stream add the liquid sugar to the egg whites until well mixed
- Take half of the egg white topping and add to the filling mix
- Lightly fold in and pour the filling into the pie shell
- Bake for 20 minutes at 350°F (177°C) then remove from oven
- Give the remaining egg white a little whisk and spread on the top of cooked pie
- Cook for 5 minutes more, making sure it doesn't burn, the tips should be a golden brown

Serves 8

Coconut Pie

by Elvi's Kitchen, San Pedro, Ambergris Caye

Ingredients

1 pie crust
1 coconut, peeled and grated
1 tablespoon corn starch
1 egg yolk
$1/2$ teaspoon lemon peel, grated
1 teaspoon lemon juice
1 tablespoon vanilla
2 tablespoons sugar
$1/4$ cup condensed milk
$1/4$ cup evaporated milk

Preparation

• Whisk all ingredients together and pour into pie crust
• Bake at 350°F (177°C) until set

Serves 8

Drinks

chaya Drink

by Franco's Restaurant, Luba Hati, Placencia Penninsula

Ingredients

6 chaya leaves
1 lime with rind cut into small pieces
2 teaspoons honey or sugar
a few ice cubes and $1^1/2$ cups water

Preparation

• Place all ingredients in blender and blend well
• Strain into tall glasses and enjoy!

Serves 2

Note
You can add or substitute pineapple or other juices for some of the water

Pine-Mint Blender Drink

by Suzi Mickler, Maya Mountain Lodge, Cayo

Ingredients

6 large mint leaves
2 cup water or whey from yogurt
2 tablespoons honey
2 tablespoons pineapple, chopped
pinch cinnamon

Preparation

• Blend ingredients well and serve immediately

Serves 2

Melon Drink

by Suzi Mickler, Maya Mountain Lodge, Cayo

Ingredients

1 cup cantaloupe
$1/2$ cup yogurt
$1/2$ cup water
1 tablespoon honey
10 drops mint flavor (or two mint leaves)
8 ice cubes

topping: 2 tablespoons whipped cream

Preparation

• Blend ingredients well and serve immediately with topping

Serves 2

Bean Drink
(like cold bean Soup)

by Suzi Mickler, Maya Mountain Lodge, Cayo

Ingredients

1/3 cup well cooked black beans
1/2 teaspoon oil
1/2 clove garlic
2/3 teaspoon Worcestershire
salt to taste
Add cilantro, parsley, or other fresh herbs if you wish

Preparation

• Blend ingredients with 1 cup water

Serves 2

Joker's Okra Shake

by New Joker Restaurant, Belize City

Ingredients

1/4 lb. fresh okra
1 teaspoon grated nutmeg
3 cups water
1 small tin evaporated milk
sugar or honey to taste

Preparation

• Cut up okra
• Place in a blender with nutmeg, water and milk
• Blend thoroughly
• Add sugar or honey to taste

Serves 4

Pink Lemonade

by Masanori Kondo, Cayo Centre for Employment Training, San Ignacio

Ingredients

3 large grapefruits
2 large limes
3 tablespoons honey

Preparation

• Cut grapefruit and lime in half and press juice out of them
• Add the honey to the juices and mix well
• Put ice in a glass and pour in the lemonade
• Serve it with small slice of lime

Serves 2

Lemon Grass Tea

by Felicia Nuñez from her book Gifts From My Heart and My Firehearth

Ingredients

6 stalks of lemon grass (fever grass)
6 lime leaves
6-8 cups of water
sugar

Preparation

• Boil water and add the stalks of lemon grass, tied together in a bundle
• Add the lime leaves and let tea steep for 10-15 minutes
• Pour and sweeten to taste with sugar

Serves 2

Note
Lemon grass tea is also used medicinally for fevers, coughs, colds and as a pleasant tonic beverage.

Wango Mango Float

by Chef Sean Beaton, Catering by Design, Gales Point Manatee

Ingredients

1 cup mango, peeled and diced (or ripe cantalope can be used)
1 bottle of Sprite or ginger ale
1/2 cup orange juice
1 scoop of vanilla or mango ice cream
ice cubes
whipped cream and mango wedges for garnish

Preparation

• In a blender combine mango and orange juice
• Stir in Sprite or ginger ale, slowly mixing with a wood spoon
• Pour into 2 tall glasses
• Add ice cubes, then top with ice cream, whipped cream and a mango wedge
• Share it with a friend!

Serves 2

Coconut-Mangerine Dream

by Chef Sean Beaton, Catering by Design, Gales Point Manatee

Ingredients

2 teaspoons Coco Lopez or coconut cream liqueur
1 cup coconut milk (canned)
2 teaspoons sugar
$1/2$ cup juice from mangerine, mandarin orange or regular orange
$1/2$ cup ice
$1/2$ teaspoon vanilla extract

Preparation

• In a blender combine all ingredients, blend well
• Pour into 2 tall glasses, get in a hammock made for two, sip slowly enjoying a Belizean sunset

Serves 2

Blue Hole Drink

by Seaside Cabañas, Caye Caulker

Ingredients

2 ounces "One Barrel" rum
2 tablespoons coconut cream
3/4 cup pineapple juice
2 ounces blue Curaçao

Preparation

• Add ice and blend
• Add a cherry on the top and an umbrella on the side

Serves 2

Turquoise Margarita

by Kenrick Theus, Lamanai Outpost Lodge, Indian Church, Orange Walk

Ingredients

6 lime slices
coarse salt
1 1/4 cups margarita mix
3/4 cup tequila
1/4 cup blue Curaçao
1/2 lime cut in quarters
4 cups ice

Preparation

• Rub lime around rim of 6 stemmed glasses and dip rim of glasses into salt
• Combine margarita mix, tequila, and Blue Curaçao in a blender
• Add the half lime (in quarters) and blend until lime is minced
• Add ice and blend until thick and smooth
• Pour into the 6 salted glasses and garnish with lime slices

Serves 6

Note
The Blue Curaçao gives it color and fresh lime gives it the lift! To create a sharp contrast in color, food colouring could be mixed with the salt to created a beautifully colored rim for the glasses.

Belize Rum Freeze

by Felicia Nuñez from her book Gifts From My Heart and My Firehearth

Ingredients

1 cup coconut milk
2 large bananas cut in chunks
juice of 2 limes
1 cup rum
1 cup orange juice
2 cups ice cubes

Preparation

• Blend all ingredients in electric blender
• Add more ice if necessary (drink should be slushy)

Serves 2

Chan Chich Coffee

by Chan Chich Lodge, Gallon Jug

Ingredients

2 ounces brandy
2 ounces Bailey's Irish Cream
1 1/2 cups Gallon Jug coffee, freshly brewed
2 tablespoons whipped cream for garnish

Preparation

• Add brandy and Baileys to cup
• Pour hot coffee on top
• Top with whipped cream for garnish
• Serve in 2 tall glass cappuccino cups

Serves 2

Note
You can use Belize's own Gallon Jug shade grown coffee.

Maya Coffee

by Chan Chich Lodge, Gallon Jug

Ingredients

2 ounces brandy
2 ounces Crème de Cacao
1^1/2 cups Gallon Jug coffee, freshly brewed
whipped cream and cocoa powder for garnish

Preparation

• Add brandy and Crème de Cacao to cup
• Pour hot coffee on top
• Top with whipped cream for garnish
• For additional garnish, sprinkle lightly with cocoa powder
• Serve in 2 tall glass cappuccino cups

Serves 2

Glossary

Achiote - This hard seed from the annatto tree, is pounded into a powder or made into a paste. It has a mild, earthy flavor and is used as the red base for recado.

Adobo - A sauce or paste made from a variety of ingredients that may include chiles, salt, vinegar, garlic, and herbs.

Al dente - Describes foods, especially pasta, cooked only until soft enough to eat, but not overdone. The Italian translation is "to the teeth."

Allspice - Native to the Caribbean and South America, this spice is similar in taste to a combination of nutmeg, cinnamon, and cloves.

Béchamel Sauce - A white sauce made from butter, flour, and milk.

Belikin - Belizean beer

Bouquet Garni - Sprigs or leaves of herbs, usually bay leaves, parsley, and thyme, either tied together or placed in a cheesecloth bag and used to flavor broth, soups, and stews.

Breadfruit - This soft fleshy fruit with green, dimpled skin, can be cooked as a vegetable or baked into puddings and pies. Breadfruit was brought to the Caribbean from the South Pacific on Captain Bligh's ill fated voyage on the Bounty.

Broil - To cook by placing directly under flame in the broiler part of oven.

Bulghur Wheat - Wheat kernels that are often used in Middle Eastern and Mediterranean dishes.

Calaloo (*Amaranthus dubius,* also known as pigweed and quelite) can be cooked as a vegetable and used as a substitute for spinach. It grows wild or can be cultivated very easily, growing up to 6 feet tall.

Cassava - A long, starchy tuber used as a staple food in the Caribbean. The fibrous tubers must either be cooked or pressed to remove the prussic acid before eating. The Garifuna grate cassava and strain the pulp to make flour which they bake into bread.

Ceviche - A seafood dish made by marinating raw fish, conch, etc. in lime juice.

Chaya - The leaf of this plant can be used as vegetable or drink and is exceptionally rich in vitamins and minerals.

Chayote - This small, pear shaped, squash is usually green in color, watery in texture and mild in taste. It can be eaten raw in salads, including the seed, or cooked as a vegetable. It is also called cho-cho or christophene.

Chiffonade - **A** stack or roll of leaves, thinly sliced.

Chipotle - A chili pepper.

Cho-cho - See **Chayote**

Chorizo - A highly spiced, coarsely ground pork sausage, widely used in Spanish and Mexican cooking.

Cilantro - A pungent, leafy herb resembling flat-leaf parsley. It is sometimes called Chinese parsley, Coriander, or Mexican parsley. It is best used fresh but is also available dried.

Coco - A starchy, white tuber with shaggy, brown skin. Cut and peel just before cooking as they discolor quickly.

Conch - A large mollusc with a beautiful conical shell. The meat is quite tough if not beaten to tenderize before cooking.

Consommé - A strong, clear meat soup.

Cracked Wheat - see **Bulghur Wheat**

Crème Brûlée - A custard style dessert.

Croutons - Bread cut in cubes, drizzled with olive oil and herbs and baked until golden. Often used as a garnish for salads and soups.

Devein - To remove the vein from the back of shrimp or to remove the interior ribs from peppers.

Dredge - To coat food with a dry mixture (seasoned flour or crumbs), either by sprinkling, rolling, or shaking the food in a bag with the flour or other ingredients.

Dukunu - see **Tamalitos**

Escabeche - A hearty soup, usually served as a main dish, made with large amounts of onions, and chicken or fish.

Feta Cheese - A white Greek cheese with a strong flavor.

Habanero - An extremely hot chili pepper with a slightly "fruity" flavor, ranging in color from green to bright orange. The habanero is often used in sauces.

Hummus - A thick paste made from chickpeas and spices.

Jalapeño - A mild hot pepper, usually green in color.

Jicama - A brown-skinned root vegetable with a crunchy white flesh and mildly sweet flavor, jicama is eaten both raw and cooked.

Julienne - To cut food into thin, matchstick strips. Julienne strips are usually about 1/8 inch thick, but the length varies.

Lemongrass - a grasslike herb with lemon flavor. When boiled in a tea it is delicious and medicinal. It is known as fever grass in Belize.

Masa - A flour made from dried corn kernels which have been cooked in limewater, then left to soak overnight. The corn is ground while still wet. The dough is used to make corn tortillas.

Media Crema - This is a thick cream sold in cans in Belize.

Mirepoix - Diced vegetable blend used to cover or as a base for cooking roasts (meat, poultry or fish). Should be prepared just before using.

Okra - A vegetable brought to the Americas by African slaves. Okra pods are green and ridged. When cooked, okra gives off a viscous substance which may serve as a thickener in some dishes. Often called okro in Belize

Parboil - To boil a food briefly, until partially done. A food might be parboiled before adding it to faster-cooking ingredients to insure all ingredients are evenly cooked.

Pâté - This appetizer usually consists of seasoned, finely ground or strained meat, poultry, or fish, cooked in a crust or mold (terrine) and is often served on crackers.

Peppers - Members of the Capsicum family, some are hot, (habaneros, jalapeños and the tiny yet powerful bird peppers) or mild (also called sweet peppers, bell peppers and green peppers).

Pibil - Yucatec Maya cooking method using a pit lined with hot stones and coals, and covered with banana leaves, hot stones and dirt. Chicken, meat, fish, etc. is wrapped in banana leaves and placed in the pit to bake for several hours until very tender.

Pico de Gallo - Salsa served as a side dish with many Belizean dishes.

Plantain - A large member of the banana family. When cooked green the flavor is fairly bland, like a potato, when fried ripe, as an accompaniment to rice and beans, they are very sweet. They discolor quickly when peeled.

Polenta - A dish made of corn meal cooked with water and beaten until stiff.

Portobello - A large mushroom with a meaty flavor.

Protemas - Soy product used as a meat substitute.

Queso Blanco - A white cheese similar to farmer's cheese, it is firm enough to slice or crumble, and may be eaten as is or used in cooking.

Ramekin - A small baking dish resembling a soufflé dish, a ramekin usually measures from three to six inches in diameter and is used for individual servings.

Recado - Spice paste mixture made of achiote (also known as annatto or the lipstick plant), pepper, etc., ground together and used to season and color meat and chicken before cooking.

Roux - Melted butter with flour gradually added and cooked until golden and used to thicken various sauces and soups.

Salsa - Spanish for "sauce", salsa may be made with a variety of ingredients and may be fresh or cooked. Green salsa, usually made with green tomatoes and green chile, is called "salsa verde".

Salsa Casera - A salsa with tomatoes, onion and pepper, sold in small cans.

Sauté - To cook quickly in a pan on top of the stove until the food is browned.

Sauté Pan - A small, shallow pan used for sautéeing.

Score - To cut shallow slashes into meat, chicken or fish, usually for decoration, or to allow seasonings to enter, or excess fat to drain, or to help tenderize.

Sere - A gravy or broth, often made with coconut milk, used for cooking meat or fish.

Sesame Seeds - Crispy little seeds with a nutty flavor, used raw or roasted in savory dishes or desserts, or sprinkled on baked foods.

Soybeans - A bean that is high in protein, and used in making meat substitutes, soy sauce and tofu.

Soy Sauce - Sauce made of fermented soybeans and used in many Asian dishes, it can be bought in various strengths, from light in flavor to thick, dark and strong.

Sweet Peppers - A term which usually describes a variety of mild peppers. Bell peppers, green peppers, pimientos, and banana peppers are all sweet peppers.

Tahini - A paste made from sesame seeds, used in Middle Eastern cooking.

Tamale - Served as a snack, main meal or party food, tamales are made of a filling placed in a soft corn (masa) dough, wrapped in plantain leaves, tied and steamed until cooked. The filling may contain chicken or meat in a rich sauce.

Tamalitos - Also called dukunu in Belize, these are like small tamales, but are made of fresh corn wrapped in corn husks and are often unfilled. Usually made for parties and special occassions.

Tofu - Soy bean curd, high in protein, mild in flavor, used in many Asian dishes and as a meat substitute in vegetarian dishes.

Vinaigrette - A simple mixture of oil and vinegar with added herbs and spices, often used on salad greens or other vegetables.

Whey - The liquid which separates from the solids when cheese is made.

Wok - A large round bottomed pan used for stir-frying.

Worcestershire Sauce - A thin and dark with a piquant flavor used to season meat, gravy, sauces, and other dishes. Ingredients usually include vinegar, tamarind, onions, molasses, garlic, soy sauce, lime, anchovies, and seasonings.

Yam - A thick vine tuber grown and eaten in South and Central America and parts of Asia and Africa. Yams may be used in most recipes which call for sweet potatoes.

Yogurt - Yogurt is cultured milk which has been fermented by keeping it at a temperature of 110 degrees for several hours. The final product is creamy with a slightly tart taste. It can be used in cooking or eaten plain, with flavors, or as a frozen dessert.

Index